Evelyn Waugh:

A Checklist of

Primary and Secondary

Material

Evelyn Waugh:
A Checklist of
Primary and Secondary
Material

by
Robert Murray Davis
Paul A. Doyle
Heinz Kosok
Charles E. Linck, Jr.

The Whitston Publishing Company
Incorporated
Troy, New York
1972

Library of Congress Catalog Card Number: 77-155725

ISBN 0-87875-021-5

Printed in the United States of America

TABLE OF CONTENTS

Introduction   iii

Works by Evelyn Waugh

Books and Monographs (Items 1-37)   1

Contributions to Books (38-105)   9

Contributions to Periodicals

Fiction (106-153) 18

Nonfiction (154-380) 22

Reviews of Books (381-554) 42

Play and Movie Reviews (555-561) 59

Verse (562-567) 60

Letters to the Editor (568-657) 60

Interviews (664a-665) 68

Broadcasts (666-667) 69

Remarks (668-688) 69

Debates (689-716) 71

Drawings, Bookplates, and Dust-Jacket Designs (717-787) 75

Editor and Staff Member (781-787) 80

Miscellaneous (788-795) 81

Works about Evelyn Waugh

Bibliographies (796-815)   83

Books and Monographs (816-826)   85

Dissertations (827-841)   88

General Commentary (842-1305)   90

Articles on and Reviews of Individual Works (1306-2107) 133

Index 189

INTRODUCTION

Despite the efforts of many students and collectors, there has never until now been anything like a comprehensive list of materials by and about Evelyn Waugh. Fifteen years ago, Paul A. Doyle published the checklist from which all others stem, but it was admittedly incomplete even for the period before 1956. Five years later, Charles E. Linck added many items in the bibliography of his dissertation (itself an invaluable source-book for material about Waugh's public life), and part of his material was published in 1964, to be followed a year later by Heinz Kosok's list of critical material on Waugh. All other checklists - - Paul Farr's the most notable - - are admittedly footnotes to these three. The material which follows not only reduces to order information currently available, but adds a good many items never before listed.

The scope and depth have been possible because the project has from its inception been a cooperative venture, drawing upon widely varied experience, interest, and sources of material. Paul Doyle has depended upon his own collection and upon the libraries of the New York area; Charles Linck's research in England turned up material not available in this country; Heinz Kosok has been able to consult continental sources; and I have worked with the Waugh papers and library at the Humanities Research Center at the University of Texas in Austin. Despite our efforts, however, this compilation is not definitive. Waugh published - - and republished - - his work in a wide variety of outlets; indexes for many of these are spotty or nonexistent; and many of them were not available to us in any form. Each of us has come across tantalizingly incomplete references to work which we have been unable to check. Fortunately, the *Evelyn Waugh Newsletter*, edited by Prof. Doyle, provides a means by which addenda and corrections can be listed without undue delay, and we welcome and in fact solicit material from other students of Waugh.

The arrangement of the items is complex but not capricious. With minor exceptions, the principle of arrangement within the sections of Part I is chronological in Part II alphabetical. Exceptions to this rule are I, B and C, which sort the material into broad and hopefully useful categories, and II, E, which arranges material on individual works chronologically according to the book's date of first publication and distinguishes for each book between articles about and reviews of it. In the interest of economy, we have used a short form of reference for reviews. The index lists proper names appearing in the titles of Waugh's works or in books reviewed by him and those of his critics. Titles of Waugh's books have also been included.

The interest and generosity of others have been remarkable, and our thanks are due to Anthony Newnham, D. Paul Farr, Jeffrey Heath, Winnifred Bogaards, Alan Clodd, William English, Yvon Tosser, D. S. Gallagher, John L. Downing, A. D. Peters, Cyril Connolly, and a host of others who, knowing of our interest, provided us with material. Mrs. Helen T. DeBolt, my assistant, gave valuable help in checking indexes; Mrs. Norlyn Shadaram of the University of Oklahoma English Department staff typed early drafts of the manuscript; the Faculty Research office of the University of Oklahoma typed the final draft, Miss Peggy Epperson typed the Index. Staff members of numerous libraries, especially those of the Interlibrary Loan department of the University of Oklahoma, rendered patient service.

Robert Murray Davis
University of Oklahoma
Norman, Oklahoma

In association with

Paul A. Doyle
Nassau Community College
Garden City, New York

Heinz Kosok
University of Marburg
Germany

Charles E. Linck, Jr.
East Texas State University
Commerce, Texas

PART I: WORKS BY EVELYN WAUGH

A. Books and Monographs

The entries in this section are arranged chronologically.
First English and American editions and, when they exist,
revised editions (all incorporating prefaces by Waugh) are noted,
but no attempt has been made to list all editions. Because there
is some confusion about the order of appearance of Waugh's early
books, the month or month and day of publication in England are
given parenthetically for full-length pre-war books.
   Titles, countries, and dates of translations are listed after
each title. This abbreviated form is sufficient to indicate the
nature and extent of Waugh's foreign public. Information about
translators and publishers can be found in the appropriate volumes of *Index Translationum*.

1   *The World to Come: A Poem in Three Cantos.* London:
      Privately Printed, 1916.

2   *P.R.B. An Essay on the Pre-Raphaelite Brotherhood, 1847-
      1854.* London: Privately Printed by Alastair Graham, 1926.

3   *Rossetti, His Life and Works.* London: Duckworth, 1928; New
      York: Dodd, Mead and Co., 1928.

4   *Decline and Fall, An Illustrated Novelette.* London: Chapman
      and Hall, 1928. (18 September); New York: Doubleday,
      Doran, 1929; New York: Farrar and Rinehart, 1929. Re-
      vised edition, Chapman and Hall, 1962.
      Translations:
      Auf der schiefen Ebene, Austria, Switzerland, 1953.
      Lady Margot, Italy, 1953.
      Auf der schiefen Ebene, Germany, 1957.
      Decadencia y Caida, Argentina, 1958.
      Jámbor Pálya, Hungary, 1962.
      Skola för Gentlemän, Sweden, 1962.
      Declin şi Prăbuşire, Romania, 1968.

5   *Vile Bodies.* London: Chapman and Hall, 1930. (17 January);
      New York: J. Cape, H. Smith, 1930 (title acquired by Farrar
      and Rinehart, 1930). Revised edition, Chapman and Hall,
      1965.

Translations:
Aber das Fleisch ist Schwach, Austria, 1951; Germany, 1959.
Cuerpos Viles, Argentina, 1958.
Corpi Vili, Italy, 1958.

6 *Labels, A Mediterranean Journal.* London: Duckworth, 1930.
   (25 September). Published in America as *A Bachelor Abroad,*
   A Mediterranean Journal. New York: J. Cape, H. Smith,
   1930 (title acquired by Farrar and Rinehart, 1930).

7 *Remote People.* London: Duckworth, 1931. (3 November).
   Published in America as *They Were Still Dancing.* New
   York: Farrar and Rinehart, 1932.

8 *Black Mischief.* London: Chapman and Hall, 1932. (1 October);
   New York: Farrar and Rinehart, 1932. Revised edition,
   Chapman and Hall, 1962.
   Translations:
   Okynniga Svartninger, Sweden, 1935.
   Diablerie, France, 1938.
   Schwarzes Unheil, Germany, 1938.
   Fechoría Negra, Spain, 1950.
   Die Schwarze Majestät, Germany, 1955, 1956.
   Misfatto Negro, Italy, 1954.
   Sort Uheld, Denmark, 1958.
   Malícia Negra, Brazil, 1963.
   Kuroi Itazura, Japan, 1964.

9 *An Open Letter to His Eminence the Cardinal Archbishop of*
   Westminster. London and Tonbridge: Whitefriars Press,
   1933. Some doubt exists that this item was published, but
   it was set in type.

10 *Ninety-Two Days, The Account of a Tropical Journey Through*
   British Guiana and Part of Brazil. London: Duckworth,
   1934. (15 March); New York: Farrar and Rinehart, 1934.

11 *A Handful of Dust.* London: Chapman and Hall, 1934. (3 September);
   New York: Farrar and Rinehart, 1934. Revised edition,
   Chapman and Hall, 1964.

Translations:
Eine Handvoll Staub, Germany, 1936, 1951, 1953, 1954.
Garść Prochu, Poland, 1937, 1959.
Una manciata di polvere, Italy, 1949.
Rasuto Fujin, Japan, 1956.
Un Puñada de Polvo, Argentina, 1959.
En Handfull Stoft, Sweden, 1961.
Prgisce Prahu (Slovene), Yugoslavia, 1961.
En Håndfuld Støv, Denmark, 1962.
Qomez Afar, Israel, 1967.

12   *Edmund Campion: Jesuit and Martyr.* London: Longmans,
       1935. (September); New York: Sheed and Ward, 1935. 2nd
       edition, Boston: Little, Brown and Co., 1946; London:
       Longmans, 1947. 3rd edition, London: Longmans, 1961.
       Translations:
       *Saat im Sturm. Lebensbéld des Edmund Campion aus
       der Zut Elizabeths von England*, Germany, 1938.
       Edmond Campion, martyr, France, 1953.
       Edmund Campion, Jesuit u. Blutzeuge, Germany, 1954.
       El Jesuita y La Reina, Argentina, 1960.
       Edmund Campion, Italy, 1966.

13   *Mr. Loveday's Little Outing and Other Sad Stories.* London:
       Chapman and Hall, 1936. (July); Boston: Little, Brown,
       1936.
       Translations:
       Mala Przechadska pana Lovedaya i inne smutne opowiadania,
       Poland, 1959.
       Hr. Lovedays Lille Udflugt Og Andre Historier, Denmark,
       1960.
       Contents:
       "Mr. Loveday's Little Outing"
       "By Special Request" [Special conclusion to the serial
           version of *A Handful of Dust*, titled "A Flat in London."]
       "Cruise"
       "Period Piece"
       "On Guard"
       "Incident in Azania"
       "Out of Depth"
       "Excursion in Reality"

"Love in the Slump"
"Bella Fleace Gave a Party"
"Winner Takes All"

14 *Waugh in Abyssinia.* London: Longmans Green and Co.,
1936. (October); New York: Longmans, Green and Co.,
1936.

15 *Scoop, A Novel about Journalists.* London: Chapman and
Hall, 1938. (May); Boston: Little, Brown, 1938; Toronto:
Ryerson Press, 1938. Revised edition, Chapman and
Hall, 1964.
Translations:
L'inviato Speciale, Italy, 1952, 1956.
Die Grosse Meldung, Germany, 1953, 1962, Austria, 1956,
Switzerland, 1953.
Press-Stopp, Sweden, 1960.
Heet van de Naald, Belgium, 1963, Netherlands, 1963.

16 *Robbery under Law, The Mexican Object-Lesson.* London:
Chapman and Hall, 1939. (June). Published in America
as *Mexico: An Object Lesson.* Boston: Little, Brown,
1939.

17 *Put Out More Flags.* London: Chapman and Hall, 1942;
Boston: Little, Brown, 1942. Revised edition, Chapman
and Hall, 1967.
Translations:
Sempre Piu Bandiere, Italy, 1949.

18 *Work Suspended.* London: Chapman and Hall, 1942.

19 *Brideshead Revisited: The Sacred and Profane Memories
of Captain Charles Ryder.* London: Chapman and Hall,
1945; Boston: Little, Brown, 1945; Toronto: Ryerson
Press, 1945. Revised edition, Chapman and Hall, 1960.
Translations:
Wiedersehen mit Brideshead, Germany, 1948, 1957, 1964.
Møte med Fortiden, Norway, 1950.
Terugkeer naar Brideshead, Belgium, 1954, Netherlands,
1957.

Car nun ne peut Mourir, France, 1959.
Retour à Brideshead, France, 1960.
*Mennyt Maailma (Kapteeni Charles Ryderin
    hengelliset ja maalliset muistelmat)*, Finland,
1960.
Ritorno a Brideshead, Italy, 1961.
Brideohead Futatabi, Japan, 1963.
Gensynet med Brideshead, Denmark, 1966.

20 *When the Going Was Good.* London: Duckworth, 1946;
    Boston: Little, Brown, 1946; Toronto: Thomas Nelson
    and Sons, 1946.
    Translations:
    Als das Reisen noch schön war, Germany, 1949.
    Viaggio in Africa, Italy, 1954.

21 *Scott-King's Modern Europe.* London: Chapman and Hall,
    1947; Boston: Little, Brown, 1949.
    Translations:
    Ferien in Europa, Austria, 1950, Switzerland, 1959.
    De Laatste Latinist, Netherlands, 1950.
    Les Invités de Bellorius, Belgium, 1955.

22 *Wine in Peace and War.* London: Saccone and Speed, Ltd.,
    1947.

23 *The Loved One.* London: Chapman and Hall, 1948; Boston:
    Little, Brown, 1948; Toronto: Smithers and Bonellie, 1948.
    Revised edition, Chapman and Hall, 1965.
    Translations:
    Il caro estinto, Italy, 1949, 1958, 1967.
    Le cher disparu, France, 1949, 1966, Switzerland, 1962.
    Elsket og Savmet, Norway, 1949, 1963.
    De Dierbare, Netherlands, 1949.
    Tod in Hollywood, Austria, 1950, Switzerland, 1950,
        1961, 1966, Germany, 1957, 1966.
    Los Seres Queridos, Argentina, 1953.
    O Ente Querido, Portugal, 1957, 1967.
    A Megboldogult, Hungary, 1959.
    Stemningsfuld Begravelse, Denmark, 1960.
    O Bem-Amado, Brazil, 1961.

Den Käre Bortgångne, Sweden, 1965.

24 *Work Suspended and Other Stories Written before the Second World War*. London: Chapman and Hall, 1949.
   Contents:
   "Mr. Loveday's Little Outing"
   "Cruise"
   "Period Piece"
   "On Guard"
   "An Englishman's Home"
   "Excursion in Reality"
   "Bella Fleace Gave a Party"
   "Winner Takes All'
   "Work Suspended"

25 *Helena*. London: Chapman and Hall, 1950; Boston: Little, Brown, 1950.
   Translations:
   Helena, Germany, 1951, 1959, Switzerland, 1951, Austria, 1953, 1956.
   Helena, Denmark, 1951.
   Hélène, France, 1951.
   Helena, Belgium, 1952, Netherlands, 1952.
   Elena, Argentina, 1956.
   Helena, Poland, 1960.

26 *Men at Arms*. London: Chapman and Hall, 1952; Boston: Little, Brown, 1952.
   Translations:
   Män i vapen, Sweden, 1953.
   Hommes en Armes, France, 1956.
   Hombres en Armas, Argentina, 1957.
   Tapre Krigere, Denmark, 1958, 1965.
   Uomini Alle Armi, Italy, 1959.

27 *The Holy Places*. London: The Queen Anne Press, 1952; New York: Queen Anne Press and British Book Center, 1953.

28 *Love Among the Ruins*. London: Chapman and Hall, 1953.

Translations:
Amor Entre Ruinas, Argentina, 1956.
Und Neues Leben blüht aus den Ruinen (Eine Liebesgeschichte aus der nahen Zukunft) Switzerland, 1957.
Amore Tra Le Rovine e altri Racconti, Italy, 1960 .

29 *Tactical Exercise.* Boston: Little, Brown, 1954.
Contents:
"The Curse of the Horse Race"
"Cruise"
"Bella Fleace Gave a Party"
"On Guard"
"Period Piece"
"Excursion in Reality"
"Mr. Loveday's Little Outing"
"Winner Takes All"
"An Englishman's Home"
"Work Suspended"
"Tactical Exercise"
"Love Among the Ruins"

30 *Officers and Gentlemen.* London: Chapman and Hall, 1955; Boston: Little, Brown, 1955.
Translations:
Officiers et Gentlemen, France, 1958.
Officerer og Gentlemen, Denmark, 1959.
Herrar Officerare, Sweden, 1959.
Ufficiale e Gentiluomini, Italy, 1960.

31 *The Ordeal of Gilbert Pinfold.* London: Chapman and Hall, 1957; Boston: Little, Brown, 1957.
Translations:
L'Épreuve de Gilbert Pinfold, France, 1958.
La odisea de Gilbert Pinfold, Argentina, 1959.
Gilbert Pinfolds Höllenfahrt, Germany, 1960, 1966.
As Desventuras do Senhor Pinfold, Portugal, 1960.

32 *Ronald Knox.* London: Chapman and Hall, 1959. In America, titled *Monsignor Ronald Knox.* Boston: Little, Brown, 1959.

Translations:
Ronald Knox, Germany, 1965.

33 *Tourist in Africa*. London: Chapman and Hall, 1960; Boston: Little, Brown, 1960.
Translations:
Un Turista en Africa, Spain, 1964, 1968.

34 *Unconditional Surrender*. London: Chapman and Hall, 1961. In America, titled *The End of the Battle*. Boston: Little, Brown, 1961.
Translations:
La Capitulation, France, 1962.
Resa Incondizionata, Italy, 1963, 1964.
Kapitulation utan Vielhor, Sweden, 1964.

35 *Basil Seal Rides Again or The Rake's Regress*. London: Chapman and Hall, 1963; Boston: Little, Brown, 1963.

36 *A Little Learning*. London: Chapman and Hall, 1964; Boston: Little, Brown, 1964.

37 *Sword of Honour*. A Final Version of the Novels: *Men at Arms* (1952), *Officers and Gentlemen* (1955), and *Unconditional Surrender* (1961). London: Chapman and Hall, 1965; Boston: Little, Brown, 1966.

B. Contributions to Books.

The items in this section are divided into two categories:
1. first appearances and 2. reprinted material. The first group
is further divided into: a) Prefaces and Introductions; b) Fiction;
c) Non-fiction. Items are arranged chronologically in each sub-
section. The second group is sub-divided into fiction and non-
fiction; entries are arranged alphabetically according to the
title.

1. First Appearances
a) Prefaces and Introductions

38 "Preface" to Francis Crease, *Thirty-four Decorative
Designs*. London: privately printed, 1927. Pp. v-viii.

39 "Foreword," to Stuart and Vera Boyle, *The Rise and Fall
of Mr. Prophitt*. London: Chapman and Hall, 1938. P. [9] .

40 "Introduction" to Christie Lawrence, *Irregular Adventure*.
London: Faber and Faber, 1947. Pp. 11-13.

41 "Introduction" to H. H. Munro (Saki), *The Unbearable Bas-
sington*. London: Eyre and Spottiswoode, 1947. Pp. v-
viii. The Century Library edition.

42 "Preface" to *A Selection from the Occasional Sermons of
Rt. Rev. Msgr. Ronald Arbuthnott Knox*. London: Dropmore Press, 1949. Pp. 7-9.

43 "Foreword" to Thomas Merton, *Elected Silence*. London:
Hollis and Carter, 1949. Pp. v-vi. Waugh also edited
this book.

44 "Introduction" to Christopher Sykes, *Character and Situation*.
New York: Alfred Knopf, 1950. Pp. vii-x.

45 "Foreword" to Thomas Merton, *Waters of Silence*. London:
Hollis and Carter, 1950. Waugh also served as editor.

46   "Forword" to William Weston, *The Autobiography of an Elizabethan*, trans. Philip Caraman. London: Longmans, Green and Co., 1955. Pp. vii-viii. Also published as *An Autobiography from the Jesuit Underground*. New York: Farrar, Straus and Cudahy, 1955. Pp. vii-viii.

47   "Introduction" to Robert Hugh Benson, *Richard Raynal, Solitary*. Chicago: Henry Regnery Co., 1956. Pp. vii-xvii.

48   "Preface" to Lord Sudley, *William: or More Loved than Loving*. London: Chapman and Hall, 1956. Pp. v-vii.

49   "Introduction" to Ronald Knox, *A Spiritual Aeneid*. London: Burns and Oates, 1958. Pp. v-ix; New York: Sheed and Ward, 1958. Pp. v-ix.

50   "Preface" to Earl of Wicklow, *Fireside Fusilier*. Dublin: Clonmore and Reynolds, 1958. Pp. vii-viii.

51   "Preface" to Eric Newby, *A Short Walk*. Garden City, N. Y.: Doubleday, 1959. Pp. 11-12.

52   "Preface" to Hilaire Belloc, *Advice*. London: Harvill Press, 1960. P. v.

53   "Preface" to Ronald Knox, *Proving God: A New Apologetic*. London: The Month, 1960. P. 7.

54   "Commentary" in T. A. McInerny, *The Private Man*. New York: Ivan Obolensky, 1962. Pp. vii-xiv.

55   "Preface" to Anthony Carson, *Travels, Near and Far Out*. New York: Pantheon, 1963. Pp. v-vi.

56   "Preface" to Daphne Fielding, *The Duchess of Jermyn Street: The Life and Good Times of Rosa Lewis of the Cavendish Hotel*. London: Eyre and Spottiswoode, 1964. Pp. 5-6; Boston: Little, Brown, 1964. Pp. 3-4-

57   "Preface" to John Galsworthy, *The Man of Property*.

Mt. Vernon, N. Y.: A. Colish for the Limited Editions
Club, 1964. Pp. v-viii.

58   ''Preface'' to Alfred Duggan, *Count Bohemond*. London:
Faber and Faber, 1964; New York: Pantheon, 1965. Pp.
5-7.

59   ''Preface'' to Lorenzo Vota, *Dopo il funerale: Dramma in una
atto*. Rome, 1966. Pp. 17-19.

60   ''Preface'' to Jacqueline de Chimay, *The Life and Times of
Madame Veuve Clicquot-Pousardin*. Reims, France, 1961.

b) Fiction

61   ''The Balance; A Yarn of the Good Old Days of Broad
Trousers and High Necked Jumpers,'' in *Georgian Stories,
1926*, ed. Alec Waugh. London: Chapman and Hall, 1926.
Pp. 253-291; New York: G. P. Putnam's Sons, 1926. Pp.
279-323.

62   ''The Tutor's Tale: A House of Gentlefolks,'' in *The New
Decameron: The Fifth Day*, ed. Hugh Chesterman. Oxford:
Basil Blackwell, 1927. Pp. 101-116.

63   ''The Tutor's Tale: Miss Runcible's Sunday Morning, An
Episode in the History of Bright-Young People,'' in *The
New Decameron: Sixth Day*, ed. Vivienne Dayrell (Mrs.
Graham Greene). Oxford: Basil Blackwell, 1929. Pp.
165-171.

64   *The Curse of the Race*, in *Little Innocents; Childhood
Reminiscences* by Dame Ethyl Smith and others. Preface
by Alan Pryce-Jones. London: Cobden-Sanderson, 1932.
Pp. 93-96. [Named ''The Curse of the Horse Race'' and
dated 1910 in *Tactical Exercise*, Little, Brown, Boston,
1954.]

c) Non-fiction

65 Comment on chivalry in *Things Have Changed*, ed. Leonard
    Henslowe. London: Philip Allan & Co., 1930. Pp. 70-71.

66 "The First Time I Went to the North," in *The First Time
    I* ..., ed. Hon. Theodora Benson. London: Chapman and
    Hall, 1935. Pp. 149-162.

67 Statement in "Authors Take Sides on the Spanish War."
    (Answers to a questionnaire issued by L. Aragon and
    others.) London: Left Review [Writers Informational,
    British Section], 1937.

68 "Sir George Sitwell" [written June 20, 1942], in Osbert
    Sitwell, *Laughter in the Next Room*. Boston: Little,
    Brown, 1948. Pp. 369-370; London: Macmillan, 1949.
    P. 349.

69 "Honeymoon Travel," in *The Book for Brides*. London:
    Forbes Publications, 1948. Pp. 51-55.

70 "Come Inside," in *The Road to Damascus* ed. John A.
    O'Brien. New York: Doubleday, 1949. Pp. 17-21.

70a "Mulled Claret," in *As We Like It*, ed. Commander K.
    Downey. London: Arthur Barker, Ltd., 1950. P. 163.

71 "On Wine," in *The Pan Book of Wine*. London, 1959.
    Pp. 9-13.

72 "First Faltering Steps - - 1. Drinking," in *The Compleat
    Imbiber 6: An Entertainment*, ed. Cyril Ray. London:
    Vista Books, 1963. Pp. 15-18; New York: Paul Eriks-
    son, 1963. Pp. 15-18.

2. Reprinted material
a) Fiction

73   "Bella Fleace Gave a Party."
Anthology of Famous British Stories, ed. Bennett Cerf
and Henry C. Moriarity. New York: Modern Library, 1952.

Bedside Book of Famous British Stories, ed. Bennett A.
Cerf and Henry C. Moriarty. New York: Random House,
1940.

My Favorite Suspense Stories, ed. Maureen Daly. New
York: Dodd, Mead, 1968.

Stories of Our Century by Catholic Authors, ed. John G.
Brumini and Francis X. Connolly. Philadelphia: Lippin-
cott, 1949; Garden City, N. Y.: Doubleday, Image Books,
1955.

Treasury of Short Stories, ed. Bernardine Kielty. New
York: Simon and Schuster, 1947.

74   *Brideshead Revisited*
"Arcadia," *Masters of Modern British Fiction*, ed.
George Wickes. New York: Macmillan, 1963.

"Charles' Holiday," *The Golden Shore: Great Short
Stories Selected for Young Readers*, introd. William
Peden. New York: Platt and Munk, 1967.

75   "Cruise," *Modern Satiric Short Stories: The Impropriety
Principle*, ed. Gregory FitzGerald. Glenview, Illinois:
Scott, Foresman and Co., 1971.

76   *Decline and Fall*, "So Good for the Boys," *Great Stories
from the World of Sport*, vol. 2, ed. Peter Schwed and
Herbert W. Wind. New York: Simon & Schuster, 1958.

The complete, revised (but original) text published by
Chapman and Hall in 1962, in *Seven Great British Short
Novels*, ed. Philip Rahv. New York: Berkley, 1963.

77 "A Handful of Dust," pp. 799-1008 in *The Woolcott Reader,*
   ed. Alexander Woollcott. New York: Viking, 1935. See
   also Woollcott's "An Afterword on *A Handful of Dust,*"
   pp. 1009-1010.

78 "Love Among the Ruins."
   Modern Satire, ed. Alvin Kernan. New York: Harcourt,
   Brace and Co., 1962.

   Modern British Short Novels, ed. Robert Murray Davis.
   Glenview, Illinois: Scott, Foresman and Co., 1972.
   Contains Davis's commentary at the end of the story.

79 *The Loved One,* "The Happier Hunting Ground," in *A Time
   to Laugh: A Risible Reader,* ed. Paul J. Phelan. New
   York: Longmans, Green and Co., 1949.

80 "The Man Who Liked Dickens."
   Alfred Hitchcock Presents 12 Stories for Late at Night.
   New York: Random House, 1961; New York: Dell, 1962.
   Verbalen die Hitchcock Koos, trans. A. J. Richel.
   Antwerp: Het Spectrum, 1964.

   *The Best of Both Worlds: An Anthology of Stories for
   All Ages,* ed. Georgess McHargue. Garden City, N. Y.:
   Doubleday, 1968.

   The Best from Cosmopolitan, ed. Richard Gehman. New
   York: Avon, 1961. The headnote indicates that the story
   was first published in September, 1933, and reprinted in
   September, 1957.

   Century of Horror Stories, ed. D. Wheatley. London:
   Hutchinson, 1935.

   "The Man Who Read Dickens," in *Rendezvous: A Prose
   Reader,* ed. John J. McShea and Joseph W. Ratigan. New
   York: Scribner's, 1958. Same as "The Man Who Liked
   Dickens."

82   "Mr. Loveday's Little Outing."
      *A Chamber of Horrors Unlocked: An Anthology of the
      Macabre in Words and Pictures*, ed. John Hadfield.
      Boston: Little, Brown, 1965.

      English Short Stories of Today, 2nd series, ed. Daniel
      M. Davin. Oxford: Published for the English Association,
      1958.

      In the Dead of Night, ed. Michael Sissons. Westminster,
      Maryland: Canterbury Press, 1961.

83   "On Guard."
      Modern English Short Stories, 2nd series, ed. Derek
      Hudson. New York: Oxford University Press (World's
      Classics), 1956.

      Tall Short Stories, ed. Eric Guthrie. New York: Simon
      and Schuster, 1959.

84   "Out of Depth," in *A Catholic Reader*, ed. Charles A. Brady.
      Buffalo, N. Y.: Desmond & Stapleton, 1947. Commentary
      by Brady, 78-79.

85   "Scott-King's Modern Europe," in *The Russell Reader*, ed.
      Leonard Russell. London: Cassell, 1956.

86   "Stitch Service," in *With a Merry Heart: A Treasury of
      Humor by Catholic Writers*, ed. P. J. Phelan. London
      and New York: Longmans, 1943.

87   "Tactical Exercise," *The Pick of Today's Short Stories*,
      ed. John Pudney. London: Odhams Press Ltd., 1949.

      As "The Wish" in *The Good Housekeeping Treasury*.
      New York: Simon & Schuster, 1960.

88   *Vile Bodies:*
      "Agatha Runcible's Motor Race," in *Best Motoring
      Stories*, ed. John Welcome. London: Faber and Faber,
      1959.

"Too, too sick-making," in *Blithe Spirits: An Anthology of Catholic Humor*, ed. Dan Herr and Joel Wells. Garden City, N. Y.: Doubleday, 1962. Pp. 177-188.

b) Non-fiction

89 "The American Epoch in the Catholic Church" *Catholic Digest Reader*. Garden City, N. Y.: Doubleday, 1952. A condensed version of the *Life* article.

    The Church in the World. St. Paul, Minn.: Catechetical Guild Educational Society, 1956. A condensed version.

    A Treasury of Catholic Reading, ed. John Chapin. New York: Farrar, Straus and Cudahay, 1957.

90 "At Debra Lebanos," in *Today and Tradition*, ed. Riley Hughes. New York: Harper's, 1960. Excerpt from *Remote People*.

91 "Awake My Soul! It is a Lord," in *Spectrum: A Spectator Miscellany*. London: Longmans Green and Co., 1956.

92 "The Capture of Campion," in *A Treasury of Catholic Reading*, ed. John Chapin. New York: Farrar, Straus and Cudahay, 1957. Excerpt from *Edmund Campion*.

93 "The Death of Painting," *The Saturday Book: No. 6*, ed. John Hatfield. London: Hutchinson and Company, 1956. Pp. 49-53.

94 "Edmund Campion," Letter to the editor of *Listener,* reprinted in J. A. Kinset, *The Campion - Parsons Invasion Plot, 1580*. London: Protestant Truth Society, 1937.

95 "A Masterly Novel," in *Encore* (Second Year), ed. Leonard Russell. London: Michael Josepth Ltd., 1963. Reprint of review of Graham Greene, *The Quiet American*.

96 "Meeting with Max," in *Encore* (Second Year), ed. Leonard

Russell. London: Michael Joseph Ltd., 1963. Reprint of "Lesson of the Master."

97   "The Only Pre-Raphaelite," in Diana Holman-Hunt, *My Grandfather, His Wives and Loves.* New York: W. W. Norton, 1969.

98   "An open letter to Hon. Mrs. Peter Rodd (Nancy Mitford) on A Very Serious Subject," *Encounters: An Anthology from the First Ten Years of Encounter Magazine,* selected by Melvin J. Lasky. New York: Simon and Schuster, 1965.

99   "An Open Letter to Hon. Mrs. Peter Rodd (Nancy Mitford) on A very Serious Subject," in *Noblesse Oblige,* ed. Nancy Mitford. New York: Harper, 1956; London: H. Hamilton, 1956.

100   "St. Francis Xavier's Bones," in *The Armchair Esquire,* ed. Arnold Gingrich and L. Rust Hills. New York: Putnam's, 1958.

101   "St. Helena Empress" in *Saints and Ourselves.* London: Hollis & Carter, 1953.

102   "Saint Helena Empress," in *Saints for Now,* ed. Clare Booth Luce. New York: Sheed and Ward, 1952.

103   "Sloth," *The Seven Deadly Sins.* London: Sunday Times Publications, 1962; New York: William Morrow Co., 1962.

104   "The Technician," in *The Maugham Enigma,* ed. Klaus W. Jonas. New York: The Citadel Press, n.d.; London: Peter Owen, [1954].

105   "Titus With a Grain of Salt," *Spectrum: A Spectator Miscellany.* London: Longmans Green and Co., 1956.

C. Contributions to Periodicals.

The items in this section are divided into six categories: fiction, non-fiction, book reviews, drama and cinema reviews, verse, and letters to the editor. Entries are arranged chronologically in each sub-section.

1. Fiction

106 "Multa Pecunia," *The Pistol Troop Magazine*, 1912, pp. 1-6. Waugh edited the magazine.

107 "Portrait of Young Man With Career," *The Isis*, 30 May 1923, p. xxii.

108 "Antony, Who Sought Things That Were Lost," *The Oxford Broom*, June 1923, pp. 14-20.

109 "Edward of Unique Achievement," *The Cherwell*, 1 August 1923, pp. 14-18.

110 "Fragments: They Dine with the Past," *The Cherwell*, 15 August 1923, p. 42.

111 "Conspiracy to Murder," *The Cherwell*, 5 September 1923, pp. 116, 118.

112 "Unacademic Exercise, A Nature Story," *The Cherwell*, 19 September 1923, pp. 152-153 -- Waugh's holograph note on copy in his scrapbook: "The rest omitted owing to blind stupidity of Editor and printer."

113 "Edward of Unique Achievement - - A Tale of Blood and Alcohol in an Oxford College," *The Cherwell*, 13 June 1925, pp. 166-169.

114 "The Hire-Purchase Marrage, an Inconsequent Version of the Love-in-a-Cottage Myth," *Harper's Bazaar* (London), 1 (December, 1929), 22-23, 98, 101. This became Chapter Five of *Vile Bodies*.

115 "The Patriotic Honeymoon," *Harper's Bazaar* (London),
    5 (January 1932), 14-15, 86 (illustrated by Nicolas
    de Molas). Renamed "Love in the Slump" for
    Mr. Loveday (1936).

116 "Seth," *Life and Letters*, 8 (March 1932), 188-227. Part
    of *Black Mischief.*

117 "An Entirely New Angle," *Harper's Bazaar* (New York),
    66 (July 1932), 22, 23, 78, 80, 82. Drawings by Gal-
    braith. Another title for "Excursion in Reality."

118 "This Quota Stuff: Positive Proof that the British can make
    Good Films," *Harper's Bazaar* (London), 6 (August 1932),
    10-11, 66, 68 (Illustrated by Nicolas Bentley). Renamed
    "Excursion in Reality" for *Mr. Loveday.*

119 "Bella Fleace Gave a Party," *Harper's Bazaar* (London),
    7 (December 1932), 12-13, 100-101 (illustrated by E.
    Betlingham Smith).

120 "Cruise," *Harper's Bazaar* (London), 7 (February 1933),
    12-13, 80 (illustrated by Nicolas Bentley).

121 "Bella Fleace Gave a Party," *Harper's Bazaar* (New York),
    67 (March 1933), 36-37, 96-98.

122 "The Man Who Liked Dickens," *Hearst's International*
    combined with *Cosmopolitan,* September, 1933, pp. 54-57,
    127-130.

123 "The Man Who Liked Dickens," *Nash's Pall Mall Magazine,*
    92 (November 1933), 18-21, 80, 82-83.

124 "Out of Depth--An Experiment begun in Shaftesbury Avenue
    and Ended in Time," *Harper's Bazaar* (London), 9
    (December 1933), 46-48, 106 (illustrated by A. E.
    Teixeira Barbosa).

125 "A Flat in London," (serial version of *A Handful of Dust),*
    Harper's Bazaar (New York), 68, in five episodes:

(June 1934), 56-57, 128-131, 133, 135, 137-138.
(July 1934), 72-73, 105-106, 109-112.
(August 1934), 56-57, 96, 100, 102, 113.
(September 1934), 88-89, 148, 152, 154, 156, 158.
(October 1934), 101, 134, 136, 138, 140, 142, 144, 146, 152.

126 ''A Flat in London,'' *Harper's Bazaar* (London), 10-11, in five episodes:
10 (June 1934), 22-24, 90, 93-98, 101.
10 (July 1934), 24-25, 78, 80-83.
10 (August 1934), 16-17, 80-86.
10 (September, 1934), 68-69, 82, 84-88.
11 (October 1934), 84, 115-123.

127 ''On Guard,'' *Harper's Bazaar* (London), 11 (December 1934), 32-33, 84, 86 (illustrated).

128 ''Mr. Crutwell's Little Outing,'' *Harper's Bazaar* (New York), 69 (March 1935), 61, 130-131. Retitled ''Mr. Loveday's Little Outing'' for collection.

129 ''Mr. Crutwell's Outing,'' *Nash's Pall Mall Magazine*, 95 (May 1935), 30-32, 79-80.

130 ''Winner Takes All,'' *Strand*, 90 (March 1936), 530-539.

131 ''My Father's House,'' *Horizon*, 4 (November 1941), 329-341. A segment from *Work Suspended*, Chapter I.

132 ''Sample from a Novel: Incident from the forthcoming *Put Out More Flags*,'' *Commonweal*, 35 (3 April 1942), 585-586.

133 ''A Home for the Connollies,'' *Lilliput*, 10 (June 1942), 465-468. A segment from the later part of *Put Out More Flags*.

134 ''My Father's House,'' *Town and Country*, 97 (August 1942), 41, 56-57. Part of Chapter 1 of *Work Suspended*.

135 "Love's Labor Lost," *Town and Country*, 98 (May 1943), 47-48, 78-80, 83-86. Another segment from *Work Suspended*, Chapter 2.

136 "Brideshead Revisited," serialized in *Town and Country*, 99 (November 1944), 83-90, and (December 1944), 99-106; 100 (January 1945), 61-68, 99-101, 117, and (February 1945), 97-104, 140-143.

137 "St. Helena Meets Constantius; a legend retold," *Tablet*, 186 (22 December 1945), 299-302.

138 "The Wish," *Good Housekeeping*, 124 (March 1947), 22-23, 319-326, 328. (Another title of "Tactical Exercise.")

139 "Tactical Exercise," *Strand*, 112 (March 1947), 45-54.

140 "Scott-King's Modern Europe" [abridged version of the novel *Scott-King's Modern Europe*], *Cornhill*, 162 (Summer 1947), 321-364.

140a "A Sojourn in Neutralia," *Hearst's International Combined with Cosmopolitan*, 123 (November 1947), 67-70, 73-74, 76, 78, 80, 83-84, 86, 88. Alternate title of *Scott-King's Modern Europe*.

141 "Bella Fleace Gave a Party," *Sign*, 27 (December 1947), 26-29.

142 "The Loved One" [preprint of the novel with an introductory article by Cyril Connolly], *Horizon*, 17 (February 1948), 76-159.

143 "The Major Intervenes," *The Atlantic*, 184 (July 1949), 34-41.

144 "Compassion," *Month* NS 2 (August 1949), 79-98. Contains material not in "The Major Intervenes."

145 *Helena* [3 extracts]. *Month*, NS 3 (June 1950): "Helena--I," 391-409; *Month*, NS 4 (July 1950): "Helena--II," 7-40;

Month, NS 4 (August 1950): "Helena - - III," 77-103.

146 "Mr. Loveday's Little Outing," *Ellery Queen's Mystery Magazine*, 18 (September 1951), 124-129.

147 "Love Among the Ruins," *Lilliput*, 32 (May-June 1953), 73-96. (This printing does not include the final paragraphs of the book version.); *Commonweal*, 58 (July 31, 1953), 410-422. (The *Commonweal* version includes the book's final paragraphs.)

148 "Apthorpe Placatus," *The London Magazine*, 1 (June 1954), 16-34. A segment from Book 1 of *Officers and Gentlemen.*

149 "Bella Fleace Gave a Party," *Ave Maria*, 94 (7 October 1961), 21-23.

150 "Major Ludovic's State Sword," *London Magazine* NS 1 (October 1961), 5-13. From *Unconditional Surrender.*

151 "The End of the Battle," *Esquire.* 56 (December 1961), 171, 264, 266-267. Episode from *Unconditional Surrender.*

152 "Basil Seal Rides Again," *Esquire*, 59 (March 1963), 74-75, 77, 79, 122, 124.

153 "Tactical Exercise," *Ellery Queen's Mystery Magazine* (October 1966), 24-34.

2. Non-fiction

154 Editorial, *The Cynic*, 21 January 1916, p. 1.

155 "Our Contemporary," *The Cynic*, 21 January 1916, pp. 4-5. Review of the *Heath Mount Magazine.*

156 With D. B., "Diary of a Prize Medal," *The Cynic*, 8 February 1916, p. 4.

157 "To a Latin Prose," *The Cynic*, 7 March 1916, p. 7.

158 "Apology," *The Cynic*, 7 March 1916, p. 8.

159 "Sufficient unto the Day or the Importance of Being Lazy,"
        The Cynic, 5 May 1916, pp. 2-6. Playlet.

160 Editorial, *The Cynic*, September 1916, p. 1.

161 With D. H., "A Pun-ishable Paragraph," *The Cynic*,
        September 1916, pp. 3-4.

162 "In Defense of Cubism," *Drawing*, December 1917. Reply
        by G. E. de M. Lewin in the following issue.

163 "The Dilettanti," *Lancing College Magazine*, December
        1919, pp. 107-108. Club manifesto.

164 "Lecture" (a report of Mr. Cook's lecture on Art before the
        Art Group of The Dilettanti Society and the Sixth Form,
        March 3, 1920, Lancing College), *Lancing College
        Magazine*, April 1920, p. 20.

165 "The Youngest Generation," *Lancing College Magazine*,
        December 1921, p. 85. Editorial. Reprinted Summer
        1966, p. 61.

166 "The Community Spirit," *Lancing College Magazine*,
        November 1921, p. 70. Editorial. Reprinted Summer
        1966, pp. 60-61.

167 "The Union" (report on "That this House deplores the
        recent Policy of the Government in the Near East and
        regrets that the Solution of the Question involved was
        not entrusted to the League of Nations"), *The Oxford
        Fortnightly Review*, 21 October 1922, pp. 13-14.

168 "The Union" (report on "That this House approves the
        Return to Party Government on Party Lines" and "That
        Continuance of British Sovereignty in India is a Vio-
        lation of British Political Ideals"), *The Oxford Fort-*

nightly Review, 4 November 1922, pp. 25-26.

169 "The Union" (report on "That in the Present Crisis of National and International Affairs a Conservative Policy is Best"), *The Oxford Fortnightly Review*, 18 November 1922, pp. 41-42.

170 "The Union" (report on "That the Introduction of Prohibition would Benefit this Country"), *The Oxford Fortnightly Review*, 2 December 1922, p. 56.

171 "Dance It - - Don't Chance It: Sic transit gloria Mundi; Great Bulldog Insurance Scheme," *The Isis*, 7 February 1923, p. 10.

172 "At the Sign of the Unicorn: Mr. Harold Acton (Editor of *The Oxford Broom*); The Last of the Poets," *The Isis*, 7 March 1923, p. 6.

173 "The National Game," *The Cherwell*, 26 September 1923, pp. 174, 176.

174 "The Union" (on "That This House approves of the support given by France to the Separatists in the Rhineland"). *The Isis*, 6 February 1924, p. 13.

175 "Wittenberg and Oxford," *The Isis*, 14 February 1924, pp. 1-2.

176 "Lost, lost, O Lost" (about his walking stick) in "The Passing Hour," *The Isis*, 20 February 1924, p. 4.

177 "The Union" (on "Shakespeare did not Intend Hamlet to be Mad"), *This Isis*, 20 February 1924, p. 19.

178 "Isis Idol No. 594: Mr. Harold Acton," *Isis*, 20 February 1924. Unsigned.

178a "The Union" ("That This House would welcome the Disappearance of the Liberal Party"), *The Isis*, 27 February 1924, p. 10.

179 "The Union" ("That Civilization has advanced since this Society first met"), *The Isis*, 5 March 1924, p. 9.

180 "We Can't Help Wondering" (about his revolver), *The Isis*, 12 March 1924, p. 4.

181 "Oxford and the Next War," *The Isis*, 12 March 1924, p. 10.

182 "The Union" ("That the Foreign Policy of Great Britain Should Aim at Constructing a European Balance of Power"), *The Isis*, 12 March 1924, p. 15.

183 "The Union" ("That France and Russia were as responsible as Germany for World War I"), *The Isis*, 7 May 1924, p. 12.

184 "The Union" ("That Immediate and Drastic Reform is needed in our so-called Public Schools"), *The Isis*, 22 May 1924, p. 34.

185 "The Union" ("That Prohibition of Manufacture and Sale of Intoxicating Liquors is in the best interests of the Country"), *The Isis*, 28 May 1924, p. 21.

186 "The Union" ("That This House deserves its doubtful Reputation"), *The Isis*, 4 June 1924, p. 16.

187 "On With the Dance, etc.," *The Isis*, 18 June 1924, p. 3.

188 (. . . . . with Alec Waugh), "Youth's Protest, the Right to Satisfy Oneself," a Letter to a Father, *The Sunday Times*, 26 October 1924, p. 11.

189 "Dante Gabriel Rossetti: A Centenary Criticism," *The Fortnightly Review*, NS 123 (1 May 1928), 595-604.

190 "The Claim of Youth or Too Young at Forty; Youth Calls to Peter Pans of Middle-Age Who Block the Way," *Evening Standard*, 22 January 1929, p. 7.

191 "Ronald Firbank." *Life and Letters*, 2 (March 1929), 191-196.

192 "Matter-of-Fact Mothers of the New Age," *Evening Standard*, 8 April 1929, p. 7.

193 "The War and the Younger Generation." *Spectator*, 142 (13 April 1929), 570-571.

194 "A Searchlight on a Classic. No. 2: *Tess*, as a 'Modern' sees it," *Evening Standard*, 17 January 1930, p. 7.

195 "Labels: An Essay on Travel," *The Fortnightly Review*, NS 127 (April 1930), 485-499. Chapter One of *Labels*.

196 "In Defense of Pleasure Cruising; An Apologia for the new Kind of Vagabondage," *Harper's Bazaar* (London), 2 (May 1930), 36-37, 99-100. *Labels*, pp. 41-52, 133-134.

197 "Labels: Port Said," *The Fortnightly Review*, NS 127 (May 1930), 627-639, *Labels*, pp. 73-97.

198 "Gaudi," *Architectural Review* (London), 67 (June 1930), 309-311. Part of *Labels*.

199 "Labels: Malta," *The Fortnightly Review*, NS 127 (June 1930), 797-810. *Labels*, Chapter Five or pp. 116-134.

200 "Alec Waugh," *The Bookman* [New York], 71 (June 1930), 299-301.

201 "Labels, Seville, Lisbon and Home," *The Fortnightly Review*, NS 127 (July 1930), 69-77. *Labels*, pp. 196-206 or end.

202 "The Throne of Ethiopia, Tafari as King of Kings, Personal Triumph," *The Times*, 17 October 1930, pp. 15-16.

203 "Converted to Rome: Why it Happened to Me," *The Daily Express*, 20 October 1930, p. 10.

204 "The Abyssinian Coronation, Duke of Gloucester at Jibuti," *The Times*, 27 October 1930, p. 12.

205 "The Abyssinian Coronation, Duke of Gloucester's
    Arrival," *The Times*, 29 October 1930, p. 13.

206 "Duke of Gloucester in Abyssinia, Presents to the Emperor, "
    The Times, 31 October 1930, p. 14.

207 "The Statue to Menelik," *The Times*, 3 November 1930,
    p. 12.

208 "Emperor of Ethiopia, The Coronation Ceremony," *The
    Times*, 4 November 1930, p. 13.

209 "Coronation Banquet in Abyssiania, 30,000 Guests," *The
    Times*, 5 November 1930, p. 13.

210 "Emperor's Procession in Addis Ababa," *The Times*,
    6 November 1930, p. 13.

211 "The Abyssinian Festivities, Emperor's Picnic Party,"
    The Times, 7 November 1930, p. 13.

212 "Review at Addis Ababa, Capering Military Bards," *The
    Times*, 8 November 1930, p. 11.

213 "The Abyssinian Celebrations," *The Times*, 10 November
    1930, p. 11.

214 "End of Abyssinian Celebrations," *The Times*, 13 Novem-
    ber 1930, p. 13.

215 "Let Us Return to the Nineties, but not to Oscar Wilde,"
    Harper's Bazaar [London], 3 (November 1930), 50-
    51, 98.

216 "Ethiopia Today, Romance and Reality, Behind the Scenes
    at Addis Ababa," *The Times*, 22 December 1930, pp.
    13-14.

217 "Venetian Adventures," *Harper's Bazaar* [London], 7
    (October 1932), 54, 86. Illustrated by C. A. Neven
    du Mont.

218 "I Step *Off the* Map: Up the Road to Nowhere," *The Passing Show*, NS 2 (22 July 1933), 10-11. Items 218-223 a serial version of *Ninety-Two Days*.

219 "I Step *Off The* Map - - 2: Six Happy Convicts in a Great Green Prison," *The Passing Show*, NS 2 (29 July 1933), 12-13.

220 "I Step *Off the* Map: Was it a Miracle which Saved Me?" *The Passing Show*, NS 2 (5 August 1933), 8-9.

221 "I Step *Off the* Map - - 4: Nobody Asked Me - - But I Stayed the Night," *The Passing Show*, NS 2 (12 August 1933), 15.

222 "I Step *Off the* Map - - 5: The World's Worst Town," *The Passing Show*, NS 2 (19 August 1933), 12.

223 "I Step *Off the* Map - - 6: The Slaves of Fear," *The Passing Show*, NS 2 (26 August 1933), 12.

224 "Cocktail Hour," *Harper's Bazaar* [London], 9 (November 1933), 26, 87 (illustrated by Nicolas de Molas).

225 "Rough Life." *Virginia Quarterly Review*, 10 (January 1934), 70-77. Part of *Ninety-Two Days*.

226 "Farewell, 1933," *Harper's Bazaar* [London], 9 (January 1934), 52, 94 (illustrated by FISH).

227 "Abyssinian Realities: We can Applaud Italy," *Evening Standard*, 13 February 1935, p. 7.

228 "We Can Applaud Italy," *Evening Standard*, 25 February 1935.

229 "In Quest of the Pre-War Georgian," *Harper's Bazaar* [London], 12 (May 1935), 50-51, 130-132 (illustrated by Gerald Backhouse).

230 "Lines for the Jubilee," *Harper's Bazaar* [New York], 69 (May 1935), 96, 196-197.

231 "Abyssinia," *The Beda Review* [Rome], June 1935. This article summarized in *The Catholic World*, 141 (September 1935), 740-741.

232 "War Certain in Few Weeks," *Daily Mail*, 24 August 1935, p. 9.

233 "Evelyn Waugh Watches Abyssinians Training," *Daily Mail*, 27 August 1935, p. 9.

234 "Drilling the Emperor's Volunteers, French Digging in Abyssinia," *Daily Mail*, 29 August 1935, p. 10.

235 "Rains Ending in Abyssinia, Water Courses Dry," *Daily Mail*, 29 August 1935.

236 "French Count's Arrest in Abyssinia, Charged with wife as a spy, 12 Suspected Natives Captured in the Bush," *Daily Mail*, 2 September 1935, p. 7.

237 "Evelyn Waugh on Abyssinian Troop Movements, Abyssinians Entrenching, Italian Invasion Rumour Denied," *Daily Mail*, 3 September 1935, pp. 11, 12.

238 "Abyssinians Move to the 'Front,' Crowded Trains Leave Daily, Imprisoned Ex-Emperor's Bid for Freedom," *Daily Mail*, 6 September 1935, p. 7.

239 "British Guard at Addis Ababa, Secrecy Drama, Italian Consuls and Spy Mania," *Daily Mail*, 7 September 1935, p. 11.

240 "Italian Consuls Withdrawn, Insecurity of the Provinces," *Daily Mail*, 9 September 1935, p. 18.

241 "More Abyssinian Troops Moving, Civilians Reported Leaving two Towns," *Daily Mail*, 10 September 1935, p. 12.

242 "Germans Send Home Women, Only Five Remain," *Daily Mail*, 11 September 1935.

243 "Emperor's Raw Beef Banquet, Abyssinia's New Year Festivities," *Daily Mail*, 13 September 1935.

244 "Abyssinia Call to 750,000, Troops Robbing Farms, Disorderly Rabble," *Daily Mail*, 14 September 1935, p. 5.

245 "Emperor Sells Honours, Raising Revenue in Abyssina, 30£ For Cape Worth 8s, Chiefs Parade at Palace," *Daily Mail*, 16 September 1935.

246 "Abyssinian Troops Rebuked, Reluctant to Go to the 'Front,' British Minister Sees Emperor," *Daily Mail*, 17 September 1935, p. 7.

247 "Belgian Recruits in Abyssinia, Received by Emperor," *Daily Mail*, 18 September 1935, p. 12.

248 "Consuls Held Up, Safe Conduct Refused to Abyssinians," *Daily Mail*, 19 September 1935, pp. 11-12.

249 "Orders to Chiefs, Military Preparations to be Speeded Up," *Daily Mail*, 19 September, 1935.

250 "Empress's Departure," *Daily Mail*, 19 September 1935.

251 "Abyssinian View, Emperor Advised to Accept Terms," *Daily Mail*, 20 September 1935, p. 14.

252 "Emperor and Rome Envoy, Meet at the 'End-of-Rain' Ceremony, Only Act of Courtesy, 200 Priests in Abyssinia Thanksgiving," *Daily Mail*, 23 September 1935, p. 9.

253 "Abyssinian Mobilization Order, Signed by Emperor at Palace Council, Freedom for Prisoners if they join Army," *Daily Mail*, 24 September 1935, p. 14.

254 "Abyssinians' Luxury Gaol, Emperor opens Model Prison," *Daily Mail*, 25 September 1935, p. 18.

255 "Abyssinia Chiefs, Why They Accept the Emperor's Rule,"

Daily Mail, 26 September 1935.

256 "Abyssinia Pomp, Emperor's Review at Today's Feast," *Daily Mail*, 27 September 1935, p. 14.

256a "Emperor's Review in Storm, Abyssinian Chiefs' War Dance, Deluge at 'End of Rains' Ceremony," *Daily Mail*, 28 September 1935, p. 13.

257 "Abyssinia," *Catholic World*, 141 (September 1935), 740-741.

258 "Abyssinia Waits, Mobilization Decree at Any Moment," *Daily Mail*, 1 October 1935, p. 13.

259 "Railway Problem, Guard by French Troops Expected," *Daily Mail*, 1 October 1935.

260 "Abyssinian Ban on Wireless, A City Without News," *Daily Mail*, 2 October 1935.

261 "Emperor's Protest," *Daily Mail*, 3 October 1935, pp. 13, 14.

262 "Emperor in Dessye, Women Repair Roads for His Arrival," *Daily Mail*, 3 October 1935.

263 "Throbbing Drums Call Abyssinians to War, Warriors' Wild Rejoicing at Emperor's Summons," *Daily Mail*, 4 October 1935, p. 13.

264 "Addis Ababa Curfew, Italian Legation Isolated," *Daily Mail*, 5 October 1935, p. 11, 12.

265 "Emperor's Guards Yell for Blood," *Sunday Dispatch*, 6 October 1935, p. 17.

266 "Emperor's Guard, Ordered to Leave for Ogaden," *Daily Mail*, 7 October 1935, p. 14.

267 "Adowa's Value, Abyssinia says Not a Strategic Point,"

Daily Mail, 8 October 1935, p. 14.

269 "Women's Wish to Fight, 300 Parade in Men's Uniforms," *Daily Mail*, 10 October 1935, p. 15.

270 "Count Vinci's 'Holiday,' Italy Breaks off Relations," *Daily Mail*, 11 October 1935, p. 15.

271 "Count Vinci Leaving Today, Picking Up Consul on Way, Request to See Emperor Refused," *Daily Mail*, 12 October 1935, p. 7.

272 "Count Vinci Kept Under Guard, Refusal to Leave Consul Behind, Soldier-Rioters March to Emperor's Palace," *Daily Mail*, 14 October 1935, p. 9.

273 "Unruly Troops Denied Rifles, Forbidden to Enter Addis Ababa," *Daily Mail*, 15 October 1935, p. 9.

274 " 'Holy War' on Italians, Emperor Appeals to Priests, Traitor son-in-law Reported shot," *Daily Mail*, 16 October 1935, p. 7.

275 "Abyssinia and Settlement Talks, Cession of Provinces 'Impossible,' 'Even if Emperor agreed tribes would resist,' " *Daily Mail*, 17 October 1935, p. 13.

276 "Hunt for Ras Kassa, Reported Lost in Forest," *Daily Mail*, 17 October 1935, p. 13.

277 "War Cry to Emperor, 'Kept Back too long,' Tribes' Sword Pledge," *Daily Mail*, 18 October 1935, p. 11.

278 "Count Vinci Stays On," *Sunday Dispatch*, 20 October 1935, p. 15.

279 "Orators in Relays, Spate of Patriotism in Abyssinia," *Daily Mail*, 21 October 1935, p. 9.

280 "Exiled Minister's Return, Warrior's Welcome in Addis Ababa, 14,000 Italian Levies said to Have Deserted,"

Daily Mail, 22 October 1935, p. 9.

281 "Egyptian Prince in Addis Ababa, To Take Red Cross
    Corps to Front," *Daily Mail*, 23 October 1935, p. 9.

282 "Abyssinian Offensive Expected Today, Italians Twenty
    Miles Nearer Makale, Emperor's Council of War,"
    Daily Mail, 28 October 1935, p. 13.

283 "Ready for Test, Italian Advance a 'Route March,'
    Little Enemy Resistance," *Daily Mail*, 29 October
    1935, pp. 13-14.

284 "General Nasibu's March," *Daily Mail*, 29 October 1935,
    pp. 13-14.

285 "Breaches Made in Walls of Harar, Italian Attack Expected, "
    Daily Mail, 31 October 1935, p. 14.

286 "Abyssinians Fight Each Other, 70 Dead in Night Mistake,"
    Daily Mail, 1 November 1935, p. 14.

287 "Gloomy 'Joy Day' in Addis Ababa, Emperor Celebrates
    Anniversary of his Coronation," *Daily Mail*, 4 November
    1935, p. 4.

288 "Briton's Radio Post, Chief of Abyssinian Station," *Daily
    Mail*, 5 November 1935, p. 18.

289 "Salary Cuts in Addis Ababa, Officials 'Gifts' to Treasury, "
    Daily Mail, 7 November 1935, p. 15.

290 "Prince of 19 to Act for Emperor, Return to Addis Ababa,"
    Daily Mail, 8 November 1935.

291 Small item about silence at Addis Ababa on part of British
    and Americans, while natives march in streets, *Daily
    Mail*, 12 November 1935, p. 11.

292 "Emperor Calls a War Council, General to Come by Air,"
    Daily Mail, 13 November 1935, p. 12.

293 "Emperor's Week of Prayer, Ras Desta's Reported Offensive,"
       Daily Mail, 14 November 1935, p. 15.

294 "Abyssinian Ruler's Pledge, 'I will shed my blood for my
       People,' " *Daily Mail*, 19 November 1935, p. 9.

295 "Anarchy in Abyssinian Army Centre, Disgruntled Troops
       Loot Villages, Tribes 'Battle' Among themselves,"
       Daily Mail, 19 November 1935, p. 14.

296 "Abyssinia's Big Sicklist, Influenza Among Imperial Guards,
       Ration Shortage," *Daily Mail*, 25 November 1935, p. 7.

297 " 'Impregnable' Road to Addis Ababa, 200 Miles of Natural
       Fortresses," *Daily Mail*, 26 November 1935.

298 "Emperor on Way to Front," *Daily Mail*, 30 November 1935.

299 "The Disappointing War. I," *The English Review*, 63
       (August 1936), 114-123. Part of Chapter One of
       Waugh in Abyssinia.

300 "The Disappointing War. II," *The English Review*, 63
       (September 1936), 209-221. Part of Chapter One of
       Waugh in Abyssinia.

301 "The Disappointing War. III," *The English Review*, 63
       (October 1936), 313-326. Part of Chapter One of
       Waugh in Abyssinia.

302 "Abyssinia Re-visited," *Tablet*, 168 (17 October 1936),
       513-516. [Extract from "Waugh in Abyssinia."]

303 "Abyssinia Re-visited," *Tablet*, 168 (24 October 1936),
       551-554.

304 "The Roman Way," *G. K.'s Weekly*, 24 (19 November 1936),
       210-211. From *Waugh in Abyssinia*.

305 "Malta," *Men Only*, 3 (November 1936), 51-54. From
       Labels.

305a "Books for Christmas," *Spectator,* 157 (18 December 1936), 1077.

306 "Christmas at Bethlehem," *Tablet,* 168 (19 December 1936), 861.

307 "General Conversation," *Nash's Pall Mall Magazine,* 98 (March 1937), 8-9.

308 "General Conversation: In preparation . . . Hostesses and housebreakers get ready for the Coronation," *Nash's Pall Mall Magazine,* 99 (April 1937), 8, 10-11.

309 "General Conversation: Gilded Youth," *Nash's Pall Mall* 99 (May 1937), 8, 10-11.

310 "General Conversation: Cad Architecture," *Nash's Pall Mall Magazine,* 99 (June 1937), 8, 10-11.

311 "General Conversation: Barabbas, Publisher," *Nash's Pall Mall Magazine,* 99 (July 1937), 8, 10-11.

312 "General Conversation: Variety," *Nash's Pall Mall Magazine,* 99 (September 1937), 8-9.

313 "From London to Budapest, British and Irish Pilgrims Welcomed in European Countries," *Catholic Herald* [London], 27 May 1938, p. 1.

314 "Impressions of Splendour and Grace," *Catholic Herald,* 3 June 1938, pp. 1, 9.

315 "Well-Informed Circles, . . . And How to Move in Them," *Vogue* [U.S.], 93 (1 April 1939), 90-91, 127.

316 "Religion in Mexico, Impressions on a Recent Visit. I. The Straight Fight," *Tablet,* 173 (29 April 1939), 543-545. Items 316-320 from *Robbery Under Law.*

317 "Religion in Mexico, Impressions on a Recent Visit. II," *Tablet,* 173 (6 May 1939), 575-576.

318 "Religion in Mexico, Impressions on a Recent Visit. III," *Tablet*, 173 (13 May 1939), 606-607.

319 "Religion in Mexico, Impressions on a Recent Visit. IV," *Tablet*, 173 (20 May 1939), 638-639.

320 Excerpt from *Mexico: An Object Lesson, Cathloic Digest*, 5 (February 1941), 49-56.

321 "Commando Raid on Bardia," *Life*, 11 (17 November 1941), 63-66, 71, 72, 74. Abridged in *The Reader's Digest*, 40 (February 1942), 122-125.

322 "Hilary A. St. George Saunders," *Book-of-the-Month Club News*, May 1943, pp. 5-6.

324 "Fan-Fare," *Life*, 20 (8 April 1946), 53, 54, 56, 58, 60. Abridged in *The Catholic Digest*, 10 (June 1946), 80-83; comment by *Time*, 47 (8 April 1946), 67.

324a "Palinurus in Never-never-land," *Tablet*, 188 (27 July 1946), 46.

325 "What to Do with the Upper Classes," *Town and Country*, 101 (1 September 1946), 141, 260-261.

326 "College for Martyrs," *Catholic Digest*, 10 (September 1946), 13-15. Excerpt from *Edmund Campion*.

327 "Hospitality of Campion Hall," *Tablet*, 188 (26 October 1946), 211.

328 "The Jesuit Who Was Thursday," *Tablet*, 188 (21 December 1946), 338-339; *Commonweal*, 45 (21 March 1947), 558-561.

329 "Why Hollywood is a Term of Disparagement," *Daily Telegraph and Morning Post*, 30 April 1947, p. 4.

330 "What Hollywood Touches It Banalizes," *Daily Telegraph and Morning Post*, 1 May 1947, p. 4.

331 "Death in Hollywood," *Life*, 23 (29 September 1947), 73-74, 79-80, 83-84. Abridged in *The Catholic Digest*, 12 (December 1947), 54-59.

332 "Half in Love with Easeful Death," *Tablet*, 190 (18 October 1947), 246-248.

333 "The Scandinavian Capitals: Contrasted Post-War Moods," *Daily Telegraph and Morning Post*, 11 November 1947, p. 4.

334 "Scandinavia Prefers a Bridge to an Eastern Rampart," *Daily Telegraph and Morning Post*, 13 November 1947, p. 4.

335 "The Man Hollywood Hates," *Evening Standard*, 13 November 1947. On Charlie Chaplin's *Monsieur Verdoux*.

336 "Mgr. Ronald Knox," *Horizon*, 17 (May 1948), 326-338.

337 "Let My Pulse Alone," *Vogue*, 112 (July 1948), 68-69.

338 "Hollywood is a Term of Disparagement," *New Directions in Prose and Poetry*, 10 (1948), 34-41.

339 "The Amenities in America," *The Atlantic*, 183 (January 1949), 79-80. Review article on *Vogue's Book of Etiquette*.

340 "Kicking Against the Goad," *Commonweal*, 49 (11 March 1949), 534, 536.

341 "Foreword" to Thomas Merton, "Elected Silence," *Month*, NS 1 (March 1949), 158-159.

342 "The American Epoch in the Catholic Church," *Life*, 27 (19 September 1949), 135-138, 140, 143, 144, 146, 149-150, 152, 155. *Month*, NS 2 (November 1949), 293-308. Abridged in *The Catholic Digest*, 14 (December 1949), 55-62.

343 "A Progressive Game," *Listner*, 45 (31 May 1951), 872-873.

344 "Nancy Mitford," *Book-of-the-Month Club News*, September 1951, pp. 8, 10.

345 "Books of the Year Chosen by Eminent Contemporaries," *Sunday Times*, 23 December 1951, p. 3.

346 "The Plight of the Holy Places," *Life*, 31 (24 December 1951), 58-65.

347 "Saint Helena Empress," *Month*, NS 7 (January 1952), 7-11.

348 "The Defense of the Holy Places," *Month*, NS 7 (March 1952), 135-148.

349 "Entrez et voyez," excerpt from *The Road to Damascus*, trans. R. Jouve, *Etudes*, 273 (May 1952), 146-149.

349a "Sainte Hélene l'impératrice," trans. M. Rene-Bazin, *Etudes*, 273 (May 1952), 150-156.

349b "Urbane Enjoyment Personified," *The New York Times Magazine*, 30 November 1952, pp. 28, 71, 73. On Sir Osbert Sitwell.

349c "Prince of Enjoyment," *Sunday Times*, 7 December 1952. Same as "Urbane Enjoyment Personified."

349d "Mr. Waugh Replies," *Spectator*, 191 (3 July 1953), 23-24. On *Love Among the Ruins*.

349e "Goa: the Home of a Saint," *Month*, NS 10 (December 1953), 325-335; Same as "St. Francis Xavier's Bones," *Esquire*, 40 (December 1953), 83, 226-229.

349f "After 'Family Portrait': Selections from the Next Popular Controversy," *Punch*, 228 (25 May 1955), 632.

349g "Awake my Soul! It is a Lord," *Spectator*, 195 (8 July 1955), 36-37.

349h "Youth at the Helm and Pleasure at the Prow," *The London Magazine*, 2 (August 1955), 51-52. On Aldous Huxley, *Antic Hay*.

349j "Literary Style in England and America," *Books on Trial*, 14 (October 1955), 65-66.

349k "An open Letter to Hon. Mrs. Peter Rodd (Nancy Mitford) on a very Serious Subject," *Encounter*, 5 (December 1955), 11-17.

350 "Dr. Wodehouse and Mr. Wain," *Spectator*, 196 (24 February 1956), 243-244.

351 "Robert Hugh Benson," *Books on Trial*, 14 (April-May 1956), 341-342, 386.

352 "Lesson of the Master," *Sunday Times*, 27 May 1956. Same as 'Max Beerbohm: A Lesson in Manners," *Atlantic*, 198 (September 1956), 75-76.

353 "A Tribute to Ronald Knox, *Sunday Times*, 1 September 1957, p. 7.

354 "Anything Wrong With Priestley?" [article replying to J. B. Priestley's review of *The Ordeal of Gilbert Pinfold*, "What Was Wrong With Pinfold," *New Statesman*, 54 (31 August 1957), 224], *Spectator*, 199 (13 September 1957), 328-329.

355 "Ronald Knox: the Quintessence of Oxford," *Tablet*, 213 (2 May 1959), 419. (The text of a speech about Knox given at Oxford.)

356 "The Life of Ronald Knox" (Extracts from Waugh's *Life of Knox*), *Tablet*, 213 (29 August 1959), 712-714; (5 September 1959), 734-736; (12 September 1959), 758-759; (19 September 1959), 783-785; (26 September 1959),

807-809; (3 October 1959), 832-833.

357 "Aspirations of a Mugwump," *Spectator,* 203 (2 October 1959), 435.

358 "These Roman Scandals," *Daily Mail,* 11 March 1960. On *La Dolce Vita.*

359 "In the growing cult of sun-worship, I pity the helpless Briton," *Daily Mail,* 28 March 1960, p. 8. This and the next three items are part of the "Passport into Spring" series.

360 "Now, why can't Britain have a CASINO AT THE END OF EVERY PIER," *Daily Mail,* 29 March 1960, p. 6.

361 "Sinking, shadowed and sad - - the last glory of Europe," *Daily Mail,* 30 March 1960, p. 6.

362 "Thank heavens for **D. D. T.**," *Daily Mail,* 31 March 1960, p. 13.

363 "Tourist in Africa" (preprints of a travel book in six installments), *Spectator,* 205 (15 July 1960), 91-93, 95-96; (22 July 1960), 127-130; (29 July 1960), 178-181; (5 August 1960), 210-213; (12 August 1960), 243-246; (19 August 1960), 275-278.

364 "An Irishman in the Making," *The Observer,* 12 February 1961, p. 9. On Edward, Earl of Longford.

365 "An Act of Homage and Reparation to P. G. Wodehouse" (text of BBC broadcast, July 15, 1961), *Sunday Times,* Mag. Sect., 16 July 1961, pp. 21, 23.

366 "Some Rhodesian Iconographers," *Good Work,* 24 (September 1961), 57-60. Excerpt from *A Tourist in Africa.*

367 " 'Brideshead Revisited' Revisited," *The Critic,* 20 (December 1961-January 1962), p. 35. This is the preface from the revised second uniform edition of *Brideshead* (1960).

368 "Evelyn Waugh on Sloth," *Sunday Times*, Mag. Section, 7 January 1962, p. 21. Excerpt in *Catholic Digest*, 27 (March 1963), 105-109.

369 "Here they are, the English lotus-eaters," *Daily Mail*, 20 March 1962.

370 "Manners and Morals," *Daily Mail*, 12 April 1962, p. 12.

371 "Manners and Morals-2," *Daily Mail*, 13 April 1962, p. 10.

372 "Return to Eldorado," *Sunday Times*, Mag. Section, 12 August 1962, p. 17. Reprinted as "Eldorado Revisited," *National Review*, 13 (9 October 1962), 259-261.

373 "The Same Again, Please," *Spectator*, 209 (23 November 1962), 785-788.

374 "My Father," *Sunday Telegraph*, 2 December 1962, pp. 4-5. Reprinted as "Father and Son," *Atlantic*, 211 (March 1963), 48-51.

375 "The Same Again Please: A Layman's Hopes of the Vatican Council," *National Review*, 13 (4 December 1962), 429-432. Reprinted as a separate pamphlet by the *National Review*, 1962. See the replies in *National Review*, 18 December 1962, p. 486; 31 December 1962, p. 521; and 15 January 1963, p. 37.

376 "An Appreciation of Pope John," *Saturday Evening Post*, 236 (27 July 1963), 84-85.

377 "Alfred Duggan." (Text of Broadcast given on 2 July 1964), *Spectator*, 213 (10 July 1964), 38-39. Reprinted as "Alfred Duggan: In Memoriam," *America*, 111 (24 October 1964), 483-485.

378 "In Which Our Hero's Fortunes Fall Very Low" (excerpt from *A Little Learning*), *Esquire*, 62 (August 1964), 48-51.

379 "Evelyn Waugh's Impressions of Spain," *Venture*, 2 (February 1965), 58-63.

380 "Fizz, Bubbly, Pop," *Wine and Food*, no. 123 (Autumn 1964), special insert between pp. 40 and 41. Reprinted in *Vogue*, 146 (September 1965), 156, 164.

3. Reviews of Books

381 Review of Alec Waugh, *Myself When Young, Cherwell*, 10 November 1923. Unsigned.

382 "A Bald Story" [review of Alec Waugh, *Card Castle*], *Isis*, 18 June 1924, pp. 16-17.

383 "Turning Over New Leaves--A Literary Harvest Thanksgiving: A Biography, Book of Essays, Collected Poems, Dialogues and Monologues, and two Novels" [reviews of N. Douglas, *In the Beginning;* L. Housman, *Life of HRH, The Duke of Flamborough;* H. Wolfe, *Dialogues and Monologues;* B. Russell, *Sceptical Essays; The Collected Poems of D. H. Lawrence;* B. K. Seymour, *Youth Rides Out*], *Vogue* [London], 17 October 1928, pp. 59, 86.

384 "Peter Wilkins" [review of Robert Paltock, *The Life and Adventures of Peter Wilkins*, illustrated by Edward Bawden], *The Observer*, 9 December 1928, p. 8.

385 "Illustrated Books" [reviews of W. R. Fuerst and S. J. Hume, *Twentieth Century Stage Decoration;* D. Morand, *Monumental and Commercial Architecture of Great Britain;* E. B. Hovell, *Indian Sculpture and Painting;* P. Koechlin and G. Migeon, *Oriental Art;* M. Salamon, *Fine Print of the Year, 1928;* G. Smith and F. Bengar, *The Oldest London Bookshop, 1728-1928*], *The Observer*, 17 February 1929, p. 9.

386 "Cities of the Future" [reviews of Le Corbusier, *The City*

of Tomorrow; Dorothy Todd and Ray Mortimer, *The New Interior Decoration*], *The Observer*, 11 August 1929, p. 6.

387 "A Miscellany of Art Books" [reviews of Arthur Symons, *From Toulouse-Lautrec to Rodin;* Ana M. Berry, *Art for Children;* Ana M. Berry, *Animals in Art;* W. G. Raffe, *Poster Design;* Sir John Soane, *Lectures on Architecture;* Francis Carruthers Gould, *Nature Caricatures*], *The Observer*, 12 January 1930, p. 6.

388 Review of Terence Greenidge, *Degerate Oxford? The Fortnightly Review*, NS 127 (March 1930), 423-424.

389 "The Traveller" [reviews of Max Gruhl, *The Citadels of Ethiopia*, and James Childers, *From Siam to Suez*], *Spectator*, 148 (9 April 1932), 518.

390 "An Indian Comedy" [review of J. R. Ackerley, *Hindoo Holiday*], *Spectator*, 148 (16 April 1932), 562.

391 "The Cold North" [reviews of H. H. Houben, *The Call of the North* and Jan Welzl, *Thirty Years in the Golden North*], *Spectator*, 148 (18 June 1932), 869.

392 "Travellers' History" [reviews of Peter Quennell, *A Superficial Journey;* Wyndham Lewis, *Filibusters in Barbary;* Alan Pryce-Jones, *People in the South;* Jan and Cora Gorden, *Three Lands on Three Wheels*], *Spectator*, 149 (6 August 1932), 186.

393 "Travellers" [reviews of A. S. Wadia, *The Call of the Southern Cross;* Kasimir Edschmid, *South America;* George Borchner, *A Wayfarer in Denmark;* Leonard Matters, *Through the Kara Sea;* Waldo Frank, *Dawn in Russia*], *Spectator*, 149 (1 October 1932), 412, 414.

394 "Rossetti's Wife" [review of Violet Hunt, *The Wife of Rossetti*], *Spectator*, 149 (8 October 1932), 449.

395 "Travellers' Tales" [reviews of Penryn Goldman, *To*

Hell and Gone; Julian Duguid, *Tiger-Man;* Amelie
Posse-Brazdova, *Sardinian Side-show;* Lowell
Thomas, *Kabluk of the Eskimo;* Robert Gibbings,
Iorana!; Walter Bayes, *A Painter's Baggage*], *Spectator*, 149 (18 November 1932), 703, 705.

396 "Mr. Fleming in Brazil" [review of Peter Fleming, *Brazilian Adventure*], *Spectator*, 150 (11 August 1933), 195-196.

397 "Travellers" [reviews of L. M. Nesbitt, *Desert and Forest;* John Dos Passos, *In All Countries;* Gordon Sinclair, *Cannibal Quest*], *Spectator*, 153 (28 September 1934), 448, 450.

398 "A Contrast in Lives" [reviews of Albert Gervais, *A Surgeon's China*, and Rawdon Hoare, *Rhodesian Mosaic*], *Spectator*, 153 (12 October 1934), 538.

399 "History in Rhymes" [review of Geoffrey Moss, *A Box of Dates for Children*], *Spectator*, 153 (23 November 1934), 24 of The Book Supplement.

400 "East and South" [reviews of Sacheverell Sitwell, *Touching the Orient;* H. M. Tomlinson, *South to Cadiz;* Patrick Balfour, *Grand Tour;* C. G. Bruce, *Himalayan Wanderer*], *Spectator*, 153 (7 December 1934), 890, 892.

401 "An American Shocker" [review of Frances Winwar, *The Rossettis and their Circle*], *Spectator*, 154 (11 January 1935), 58.

402 "Blinding the Middle-Brow" [review of Aldous Huxley, *Eyeless in Gaza*], *Tablet*, 168 (18 July 1936), 84.

403 "Engineer-Author" [review of L. M. Nesbitt, *Desolate Marches*], *Spectator*, 155 (19 July 1935), 106.

404 "White Trash" [review of Marcelle Prat, *White, Brown and Black*], *Spectator*, 155 (26 July 1935), 164, 166.

405 "Undiscovered Asia" [review of Peter Fleming, *News from Tartary*], *Spectator*, 157 (7 August 1936), 244.

406 "Disappointing War" [review of Ladislas Farago, ed. *Abyssinian Stop Press*], *Spectator*, 157 (2 October 1936), 554.

407 "An English Humorist" [review of P. G. Wodehouse, *Laughing Gas*], *Tablet*, 168 (17 October 1936), 532-533.

408 "Abyssinian Aftermath" [review of Mortimer Durand, *Crazy Campaign*], *Tablet*, 168 (28 November 1936), 784.

410 "A *Times* Correspondent" [review of G. L. Steer, *Caesar in Abyssinia*], *Tablet*, 169 (23 January 1937), 128-129.

411 "Through European Eyes" [review of Marshal de Bono, *Anno XIIII*], *The London Mercury and Bookman*, 36 (June 1937), 147-150.

412 "A Mystic in the Trenches" [review of David Jones, *In Parenthesis*; Margaret Barton, *Tunbridge Wells*; E. C. Large, *Sugar in the Air*; G. E. Trevelyan, *Two Thousand Million Man-Power*], *Night and Day*, 1 (1 July 1937), 32-33.

413 "Civilization and Culture" [reviews of Christopher Sykes, *Strange Wonders*, and Robert Byran, *The Road to Oxiana*], *Spectator*, 159 (2 July 1937), 27-28.

414 "For Schoolboys Only" [reviews of C. Day Lewis, *The Mind in Chains*; Murray Constantine, *Swastika Night*; A. L. Rowse, *Sir Richard Grenville of the Revenge*; William Teiling, *The Pope in Politics*; Julius Lips, *The Savage Hits Back*], *Night and Day*, 1 (8 July 1937), 24-25.

415 "Uplift in Arabia" [reviews of Owen Rutter, *Triumphant*

Pilgrimage; M. Sandoz, *Old Jules;* Herbert Clyde
Lewis, *Gentleman Overboard*], *Night and Day*, 1
(15 July 1937), 25-26.

416 "Bonhomie in the Saloon Bar" [reviews of Peter Chamberlain, *Sing Holiday;* Paul Cohen Portheim, *The Spirit
of Paris;* John Drinkwater, *Robinson of England*],
Night and Day, 1 (22 July 1937), 24-25.

417 "The Soldiers Speak" [review of Guy Chapman, *Vain
Glory*], *Night and Day*, 1 (29 July 1937), 24-25.

418 "The Great Incomprehensibles" [review of E. T. Bell,
Men of Mathematics], *Night and Day*, 1 (5 August
1937), 23-24.

419 "Bloomsbury's Farthest North" [reviews of W. H. Auden
and Louis MacNeice, *Letters from Iceland;* Philip
Thornton, *Dead Puppets Dance*], *Night and Day*, 1
(12 August 1937), 25-26.

420 "Folkestone, for Shame!" [review of Netta Muskett,
Middle Mist], *Night and Day*, 1 (19 August 1937), 24-
25.

421 "Uplift in the Highball" [reviews of Horace McCoy,
No Pockets in a Shroud; Michael Arlen, *The Crooked
Coronet*], *Night and Day*, 1 (26 August 1937), 26-27.

422 "Companion to Fleming" [reviews of Ella K. Maillart,
Forbidden Journey; Dr. Johnston Abraham, *99 Wimpole
Street*], *Night and Day*, 1 (2 September 1937), 26-27.

423 "Peter Pan in Politics" [reviews of Arthur Calder-Marshall, *The Changing Scene;* Dave Marlowe, *Coming
Sir!*], *Night and Day*, 1 (9 September 1937), 25-26.

424 "Art from Anarchy" [review of Arthur Calder-Marshall,
A Date with a Duchess], *Night and Day*, 1 (16 September 1937), 24-25.

425 "An Old Liberal Says his Say" [review of J. A. Spender, *Men and Things*], *Night and Day*, 1 (23 September 1937), 24-25.

426 "A Teuton in Tudor England" [reviews of Clare Williams, ed., *Thomas Platter's Travels in England;* Max Miller, *Mexico Around Me;* G. E. P. Collins, *Makassar Sailing;* A. J. Marshall, *The Black Musketeers*], *Night and Day*, 1 (30 September 1937), 26, 28.

427 "Love Among the Underdogs" [reviews of Pamela Hansford-Johnson, *Worlds End;* Kenneth Allott and Stephen Tait, *The Rhubarb Tree;* Frederic Prokosch, *The Seven Who Fled*], *Night and Day*, 1 (7 October 1937), 29.

428 "Strange Rites of the Islanders" [review of *May the Twelfth: Mass Observation Day--surveys*], *Night and Day*, 1 (14 October 1937), 28, 30.

429 "Edith Sitwell's First Novel" [reviews of Edith Sitwell, *I Live Under a Black Sun;* Ernest Hemingway, *To Have and Not to Have;* Terence Greenidge, *Tin Pot Country*], *Night and Day*, 1 (21 October 1937), 28-29.

430 "Saint's-Eye View" [reviews of Georges Bernanos, *The Diary of a Country Priest;* Julian Pine, *Rotton Borough;* Eric Linklatter, *The Sailor's Holiday;* William Lamb, *The World Ends;* G. M. Young, *Daylight and Champagne;* H. E. Bates and Agnes Miller Parker, *Down the River*], *Night and Day*, 1 (28 October 1937), 24-25.

431 "All Memory Gone" [reviews of T. O. Beachcroft, *The Man Who Started Clean;* Patrick Balfour, *Lords of the Equator;* Siegfried Sassoon, *The Complete Memoirs of George Sherston;* Neil Stewart, *The Fight for the Charta*], *Night and Day*, 1 (4 November 1937), 24-25.

432 "The International List" [reviews of Ethel Firebrace, *Autobiography: Press Gang;* Leonard O. Ross, *The Education of Hyman Kaplan;* Freya Stark, *Baghdad Sketches*], *Night and Day*, 1 (11 November 1937), 23.

433 "Edwardian Baroque" [reviews of V. Sackville-West, *Pepita;* Sir Ronald Storrs, K.C.M.G., *Orientation;* Stephen Tennant, *Leaves from a Missionary's Notebook*], *Night and Day*, 1 (18 November 1937), 28, 30.

434 "A Parnassian on Mount Zion" [reviews of John Betjeman, *Continual Dew;* Charles Prior, *So I Wrote It*], *Night and Day*, 1 (25 November 1937), 24-25.

435 "Popes and Peoples" [reviews of Lord Clomore, *Pope Pius XI and World Peace;* James Laver, *Taste and Fashion;* Earl of Ilchester, *Chronicles of Holland House, 1820-1900*], *Night and Day*, 1 (2 December 1937), 24-25.

436 "Viceregal Gothic" [reviews of Harold Nicolson, *Helen's Tower;* J. B. Morton, *Sideways Through Borneo;* Hugh McGraw, *Fine Romance*], *Night and Day*, 1 (9 December 1937), 27-28.

437 "Crusader Manque" [reviews of A. F. Tshiffely, *Don Roberto;* Hesketh Pearson and Hugh Kingsmill, *Skye High*], *Night and Day*, 1 (16 December 1937), 25-26.

438 "More Barren Leaves" [reviews of Aldous Huxley, *Ends and Means;* The Right Honorable J. R. Clynes, *Memoirs;* C. P. Rodoconachi, *No Innocent Abroad*], *Night and Day*, 1 (23 December 1937), 24-25.

439 "The Oxford Arctic Expedition" [review of Alexander R. Glen and Noel A. C. Croft, *Under the Polar Star*], *Tablet*, 171 (15 January 1938), 80-81.

440 "Author in Search of a Formula" [review of Christopher Isherwood, *Lions and Shadows*], *Spectator*, 160 (25 March 1938), 538.

441 "Unfortunate Isles" [review of Archibald Lyall, *Black and White Make Brown*], *Spectator*, 160 (8 April 1938), 640.

442 "Felo De Se" [review of Henry R. Fedden, *Suicide: A Social and Historical Study*], *Spectator*, 160 (15 April 1938), 678.

443 "The Habits of the English" [review of *First Year's Work, 1937-38 by Mass Observation*], *Spectator*, 160 (15 April 1938), 663-664.

444 "The New Patriotism" [reviews of Ceciley Hamilton, *Modern England* and Beverley Nichols, *News of England*], *Spectator*, 160 (22 April 1938), 714, 716.

445 "The Irish Bourgeoisie" [review of Kate O'Brien, *Pray for the Wanderer*], *Spectator*, 160 (29 April 1938), 768.

446 "A Victorian Escapist" [review of Angus Davidson, *Edward Lear*], *Spectator*, 160 (6 May 1938), 813-814.

447 "A Guide-Book to Roumania" [review of Sacheverell Sitwell, *Roumanian Journey*], *Spectator*, 160 (20 May 1938), 924.

448 "Desert Islander" [review of Malcolm Muggeridge, *In a Valley of this Restless Mind*], *Spectator*, 160 (27 May 1938), 978, 980.

449 "Five Lives" [reviews of Lord Elton, *Among Others;* Lord Dunsany, *Patches of Sunlight;* David Edstrom, *The Testament of Caliban;* Walter Starkie, *The Waveless Plain;* John Van Druten, *The Way to the Present*], *Spectator*, 160 (17 June 1938), 1112, 1114.

450 "Fiction" [reviews of Lettice Cooper, *National Provincial;* Robert Nicolson, *Love is a Sickness;* Herbert Kahan, *Apollo Flies;* James Hanley, *Hollow Sea*], *Spectator*, 160 (24 June 1938), 1162.

451 "The New Countryman" [review of *The Country Citizen* by The Countryman], *Spectator*, 161 (8 July 1938), 54-55.

452 "Fine Ladies" [review of *The Ladies of Alderley*, ed. Nancy Mitford], *Tablet*, 172 (23 July 1938), 110-112.

453 "Six Travellers" [reviews of Herbert Tichy, *Tibetan Adventure;* John Hanbury-Tracy, *Black River of Tibet;* Dana Lamb and June Cleveland, *Enchanted Vagabonds;* Theodora Benson, *In the East My Pleasure Lies;* James Ramsey Ullman, *The Other Side of the Mountain*], *Spectator*, 161 (29 July 1938), 207.

454 "Mr. Belloc in the North" [review of Hilaire Belloc, *Return to the Baltic*], *Spectator*, 161 (2 December 1938), 964, 966.

455 "Present Discontents" [review of Cyril Connolly, *Enemies of Promise*], *Tablet*, 172 (3 December 1938), 743-744.

456 "Machiavelli and Utopia--Revised Version" [review of H. G. Wells, *The Holy Terror*], *Spectator*, 162 (10 February 1939), 234.

457 "The Technician" [review of W. Somerset Maugham, *Christmas Holiday*], *Spectator*, 162 (17 February 1939), 274.

458 "The Waste Land" [review of Graham Greene, *The Lawless Roads*], *Spectator*, 162 (10 March 1939), 413-414.

459 "Mr. Isherwood and Friend" [review of W. H. Auden and Christopher Isherwood, *Journey to a War*], *Spectator*, 162 (24 March 1939), 496, 498.

460 "An Angelic Doctor; the Work of Mr. P. G. Wodehouse" [review of *Week End Wodehouse*], *Tablet*, 173 (17 June 1939), 786-787.

461 "Good Travellers" [reviews of C. S. Jarvis, *The Back Garden of Allah;* Gerald Reitlinger, *South of the Clouds;* William J. Makin, *Caribbean Nights;* Mora Gardner, *Menacing Sun*], *Spectator*, 163 (25 August 1939), 300.

462 "Literary Lives" [reviews of J. B. Priestley, *Rain Upon*

Gadshill; Howard Spring, *Heaven Lies About Us;*
James Bridie, *One Way of Living*], *Spectator*, 163
(1 September 1939), 331.

463 "Carroll and Dodgson" [review of *The Complete Works
of Lewis Carroll*], *Spectator*, 163 (13 October 1939),
511.

464 "An Epoch-Marker" [review of Charles B. Cochran, *Cock-
a-doodle-do*], *Spectator*, 167 (19 December 1941), 582.

465 "A Trenchant Tory" [review of Douglas Woodruff, *Talking
at Random*], *Spectator*, 168 (3 April 1942), 332.

466 "Drama and the People" [review of Graham Greene, *British Dramatists*], *Spectator*, 169 (6 November 1942),
438.

467 "The Writing of English" [review of Robert Graves and
Alan Hodge, *The Reader Over Your Shoulder*], *Tablet*,
182 (3 July 1943), 8-9.

468 "Marxism, the Opiate of the People" [review of H. Laski,
Faith, Reason and Civilization], *Tablet*, 183 (22 April
1944), 200.

469 "A Pilot All at Sea" [review of Palinurus [Cyril Connolly],
The Unquiet Grave], *Tablet*, 181 (10 November 1945),
225-226.

470 "A New Humanism" [review of George Orwell, *Critical
Essays*], *Tablet*, 187 (6 April 1946), 176.

471 "Failure of a Mission" [review of Jasper Rootham, *Miss
Fire*], *Tablet*, 187 (11 May 1946), 241.

472 "Sir Osbert at School" [review of Osbert Sitwell, *The
Scarlet Tree*], *Tablet*, 188 (10 August 1946), 74.

473 "When Loyalty No Harm Meant" [review of Christopher
Sykes, *Four Studies in Loyalty*], *Tablet*, 188 (7 Decem-

ber 1946), 308-309.

474 "Felix Culpa?" [review of Graham Greene, *The Heart of the Matter*], *Tablet*, 191 (5 June 1948), 352-354.

475 "Felix Culpa?" [review of *The Heart of the Matter*], *Commonweal*, 48 (16 July 1948), 322-326. See discussion, 6 August, p. 399; 20 August, pp. 452-453.

476 "The Wet Nineties" [review of *The Eighteen-Nineties. A Period Anthology Chosen by Martin Secker*], *Month*, NS 1 (January 1949), 59-60.

477 "Pioneer! O Pioneer!" [review of J. F. Powers, *Prince of Darkness*], *Month*, NS 1 (March 1949), 215-216.

478 "Rossetti Revisited: pre-Raphaelism and Religion" [review of Helen Rossetti Angeli, *Dante Gabriel Rossetti: His Friends and Enemies*], *Tablet*, 194 (16 July 1949), 40. Reply by J. H. McNulty, 23 July, p. 58.

479 "Monsignor Knox's Old Testament; a literary opinion" [review of Ronald Knox, *Old Testament*], *Month*, NS 2 (July 1949), 41-43. Excerpt in *The Catholic World*, 170 (November 1949), 151.

480 "As Others See Us," [review of Malcolm Muggeridge, *Affairs of the Heart*], *Tablet*, 195 (4 February 1950), 91-92.

481 "An Admirable Novel" [review of Antonia White, *The Lost Traveller*], *Tablet*, 195 (22 April 1950), 314.

482 "The Happy Critic" [review of Elizabeth Bowen, *Collected Impressions*], *Tablet*, 195 (24 June 1950), 503-504.

483 Review of Ernest Hemingway, *Across the River and into the Trees*, *Tablet*, 196 (30 September 1950), 290, 292. Translation, in German, in *Universitas*, 6 (March 1951), 291-293.

484 "The Case of Mr. Hemingway" [review of *Across the River and into the Trees*], *Commonweal*, 53 (3 November 1950), 97-98.

485 "An Ideal Christmas Card" [review of Osbert Lancaster, *Facades and Faces*], *Tablet*, 196 (9 December 1950), 509.

486 "Two Unquiet Lives " [reviews of Stephen Spender, *World Within World*, and John Miller, *Saints and Parachutes*], *Tablet*, 197 (5 May 1951), 356-357.

487 "The Heart's Own Reasons" [review of Graham Greene, *The End of The Affair*], *Commonweal*, 54 (17 August 1951), 458-459.

488 "The Point of Departure" [review of *The End of the Affair*], *Month*, NS 6 (September 1951), 174-176.

489 "A Clean Sweep" [review of Angus Wilson, *Hemlock and After*], *Month*, NS 8 (October 1952), 238-240.

490 "Dream World" [review of Rex Whistler, *The Konigsmark Drawings*], *Time and Tide*, 33 (6 December 1952), 1456-1457.

491 "Mr. Betjeman Despairs" [review of John Betjeman, *First and Last Loves*], *Month*, NS 8 (December 1952), 372-375.

492 "A Self-Made Myth" [review of Vladimer Dedijev, *Tito Speaks*], *Month*, NS 9 (April 1953), 240-245. Also published in *Commonweal*, 58 (8 May 1953), 122-125.

493 "Luxurious Editions and Austere Lives" [review of Patrick Leigh Fermor, *A Time to Keep Silence*], *Time and Tide*, 34 (20 June 1953), 824.

495 "Ruskin and Kathleen Olander" [review of *The Gulf of Years. Love Letters from John Ruskin to Kathleen Olander*, ed. Rayner Unwin], *Spectator*, 191 (17 July 1953), 88.

496 "Apotheosis of an Unhappy Hypocrite" [review of Edgar Johnson, *Charles Dickens*], *Spectator*, 191 (2 October 1953), 363-364.

497 "A Fifth Study in Loyalty" [review of Christopher Sykes, *A Song of a Shirt*], *Time and Tide*, 34 (12 December 1953), 1652-1653.

498 "A Mid-Victorian Spiv" [review of Helen Angeli, *The Pre-Raphaelite Twilight*], *Spectator*, 192 (23 April 1954), 498, 501.

499 "Here's Richness" [review of *The Verses of Hilaire Belloc*], *Spectator*, 192 (21 May 1954), 622.

500 "Mr. Betjeman's Bouquet" [review of John Betjeman, *A Few Late Chrysanthemums*], *Sunday Times*, 11 July 1954, p. 5.

501 "Dropmore Press Makes Good " [review of *The Holkham Bible Picture Book*, ed. W. O. Hassall], *Spectator*, 193 (16 July 1954), 93-94.

502 "Another and Better Ruskin" [review of Joan Evans, *John Ruskin*], *Spectator*, 193 (17 September 1954), 345-346.

503 "Those Happy Homes" [review of Ralph Dutton, *The Victorian Home*], *Sunday Times*, 28 November 1954, p. 5.

504 "The Forerunner" [review of Peter Quennell, *Hogarth's Progress*], *Time and Tide*, 36 (9 July 1955), 906, 908.

505 "Belloc Anadyomene" [review of Hilaire Belloc, *The Cruise of the 'Nona'*], *Spectator*, 195 (26 August 1955), 283-284.

506 "Alfred the Little" [review of Norton B. Crowell, *Alfred Austin, Victorian*], *Sunday Times*, 4 September 1955, p. 5.

507 "The Art of Mr. Alfred Duggan" [review of Alfred Duggan, *God and My Right*], *Spectator*, 195 (18 November 1955), 667-668.

508 "The Death of Painting" [review of Helmut and Alison Gernsheim, *The History of Photography*], *Time and Tide*, 36 (3 December 1955), 1586, 1588. Reprinted in *Playboy*, 3 (August 1956), 13-14.

509 "Quixote Goes East" [review of Graham Greene, *The Quiet American*], *Sunday Times*, 4 December 1955, p. 4.

510 "Scenes of Clerical Life" [review of J. F. Powers, *Presence of Grace*], *Commonweal*, 63 (30 March 1956), 667-668.

511 "A Remarkable Historical Novel" [review of Sybille Bedford, *A Legacy*], *Spectator*, 196 (13 April 1956), 498.

512 "Journeyman to Master, Strange Case of Dr. P. G. Wodehouse" [review of *The Autograph Edition of the Works of P. G. Wodehouse*], *Sunday Times*, 3 June 1956, p. 4.

513 "A Story with a Moral" [review of Compton Mackenzie, *Thin Ice*], *Sunday Times*, 10 June 1956, p. 4.

514 "A Poet of the Counter Reformation" [review of Christopher Devlin, *Life of Robert Southwell*], *Spectator*, 196 (22 June 1956), 859-860.

515 "Something Fresh" [review of Muriel Spark, *The Comforters*], *Spectator*, 198 (22 February 1957), 256.

516 "Randolph's Finest Hour" [review of Randolph Churchill, *What I Said About the Press*], *Spectator*, 198 (22 March 1957), 369.

517 "Spicy Stories" [review of Devendra P. Varma, *The Gothic Flame*], *Spectator*, 198 (10 May 1957), 622.

518 "Unsolved Mystery" [review of Douglas Woodruff, *The Tichborne Claimant: A Victorian Mystery*], *Spectator*, 198 (21 June 1957), 816-817.

519 "Opus XV" [review of Ivy Compton Burnett, *A Father and His Fate*], *Spectator*, 199 (16 August 1957), 223.

520 "Posthumous Miscellany" [review of R. A. Knox, *Literary Distractions*], *Spectator*, 201 (17 October 1958), 523.

521 "Life and Loves" [review of Vincent Brome, *Frank Harris*], *Spectator*, 202 (20 February 1959), 268.

522 "Hands Off Smith" [review of *D. N. B.: 1941-1950*, ed. L. G Wickham Legg and E. T. Williams], *Spectator*, 202 (19 June 1959), 894-895.

523 "The Hand of the Master" [review of Priscilla Johnston, *Edward Johnston*], *Spectator*, 203 (24 July 1959), 108-110.

524 "Opus XVI" [review of Ivy Compton Burnett, *A Heritage and Its History*], *Spectator*, 203 (18 September 1959), 380.

525 "The Making of an American" [review of Leo Rosten, *The Return of Hyman Kaplan*], *Spectator*, 203 (16 October 1959), 525.

526 "The Book Unbeautiful" [reviews of Truman Capote and Richard Avedon, *Observations;* Yousef Karsh, *Portraits of Greatness*], *Spectator*, 203 (20 November 1959), 728-729.

527 "Visions and Debates" [review of C. H. Talbot, ed., *The Life of Christina of Markyate*], *Spectator*, 203 (4 December 1959), 840-841.

528 "McCarthy" [review of Richard H. Rovere, *Senator Joe McCarthy*], *Spectator*, 204 (5 February 1960), 185.

529 "Ecclesiology" [review of Peter Anson, *Fashions in Church Furnishings, 1840-1940*], *Spectator*, 204 (22 April 1960), 580-581.

530 "Marriage a la Mode--1936" [review of Anthony Powell, *Casanova's Chinese Restaurant*], *Spectator*, 204 (24 June 1960), 919.

531 "Literary Musings" [review of Peter Quennell, *The Sign of the Fish*], *Spectator*, 205 (8 July 1960), 70.

532 Review of Anthony Carson, *A Rose by Any Other Name*, *London Magazine*, 7 (September 1960), 76-77.

533 "The Only Pre-Raphaelite" [review of Diana Holman Hunt, *My Grandmothers and I*], *Spectator*, 205 (14 October 1960), 567.

534 "An Important Publication" [review of Ronald Knox, *The Occasional Sermons*, edited by Philip Caraman], *Spectator*, 205 (25 November 1960), 858-859.

535 "The Last Committed Novelist" [review of Nancy Mitford, *Don't Tell Alfred*], *London Magazine*, 7 (December 1960), 65-68.

536 "An Heroic Churchman: In the Shadow of Newman" [review of Ronald Chapman, *Father Faber*], *Sunday Times*, Magazine Section, 29 January 1961, p. 27.

537 "Chesterton" [review of Garry Wills, *Chesterton: Man and Mask*], *National Review*, 10 (22 April 1961), 251-252.

538 "Caveat Emptor" [review of Frank Arnau, *Three Thousand Years of Deception in Art and Antiques*], *Spectator*, 206 (3 March 1961), 300.

539 "British Worthies" [review of *Who's Who 1961*], *Spectator*, 206 (24 March 1961), 415.

540 "Cornucopia" [review of Daphne Fielding, *The Adonis*

Garden], *Spectator*, 206 (23 June 1961), 928.

541 "Threatened Genius: Difficult Saint" [reviews of Muriel
     Spark, *Voices at Play;* Daniel Pegeril, *Blessed and
     Poor*], *Spectator*, 207 (7 July 1961), 28-29.

542 "Footlights and Chandeliers" [review of Cecil Beaton,
     The Wandering Years], *Spectator*, 207 (21 July 1961),
     96-97.

543 "Delights of Dieppe" [review of Simona Pakenham, *Pig-
     tails and Penrod*], *Sunday Times*, Magazine Section,
     10 September 1961, p. 25.

544 "Five Years Hard" [review of Loelia, Duchess of West-
     minster, *Grace and Favour*], *Spectator*, 207 (20 Octo-
     ber 1961), 551.

545 "Last Steps in Africa" [review of Graham Greene, *In
     Search of a Character*], *Spectator*, 207 (27 October
     1961), 594-595.

546 "Bioscope" [review of Anthony Powell, *The Kindly Ones*],
     Spectator, 208 (29 June 1962), 863-864.

547 "Collector' Pieces" [reviews of R. W. Symonds and B. B.
     Whineray, *Victorian Furniture;* Elizabeth Aslin, *Nine-
     teenth Century English Furniture*], *Spectator*, 209 (19
     October 1962), 599-600.

548 "Literary" [review of V. S. Naipaul, *The Middle Passage*],
     Month, NS 29 (November 1962), 304-305.

549 "William Rothenstein" [review of Robert Speaight, *William
     Rothenstein*], *Month*, NS 29 (January 1963), 42-43.

550 "Embellishing the Loved Ones" [review of Jessica Mitford,
     The American Way of Death], *Sunday Times*, 29 Septem-
     ber 1963, p. 36.

551 "The Light that Did Not Wholly Fail" [review of *Kipling's*

Mind and Art, ed. Andrew Rutherford, and C. A.
Bodelsen, *Aspects of Kipling's Art*], *Sunday Times,*
Weekly Review, 22 March 1964, p. 35.

552 "The Man in the Mask" [review of Lord David Cecil,
Max, and *Letters to Reggie Turner by Max Beerbohm,*
ed. Rupert Hart-Davis], *Sunday Times,* 8 November
1964, p. 49. Reprinted in *Atlas,* 9 (January 1965), 47-
49.

553 "The Spirit of Edith Sitwell" [review of Edith Sitwell,
Taken Care of], *Sunday Times,* Weekly Review, 4 April
1965, p. 30.

554 "Oxford Revisited" [review of W. R. Ward, *Victorian Ox-
ford;* Christopher Halls, *The Oxford Union,* and James
Morris, *Oxford*], *Sunday Times,* Weekly Review, 7
November 1965, p. 53.

4. Play and Movie
Reviews

555 "Seen in the Dark" [review of *The Merry-go-Round*], *The
Isis,* 23 January 1924, p. 5.

556 "Seen in the Dark" [review of *If Winter Comes*], *The Isis,*
20 February 1924, p. 28.

557 "At the Super Cinema" [review of *Woman to Woman*], *The
Isis,* 27 February 1924, p. 6.

558 "The Super Cinema" [review of *The Four Horsemen*], *The
Isis,* 5 March 1924, p. 24.

559 "Titus with a Grain of Salt" [review of *Titus Andronicus*].
Spectator, 195 (2 September 1955), 300-301.

560 " 'Luther': John Osborne's New Play" [review of *Luther*],
Critic, 20, no. 4 (February-March 1962), 53-55.

561 " 'Luther': John Osborne's New Play" [review of *Luther*], reprint, *Drama Critique*, 7 (Fall 1964), 170-172.

5. Verse

562 "Ode to Sixayitiss," *The Cynic*, 7 March 1916, p. 6. Limerick.

563 Verse, *The Cynic*, September 1916, p. 5.

564 "A University Sermon to Idealists Who are Serious-minded and Intelligent," *The Cherwell*, 8 June 1922, p. 66.

565 "History Previous," *Isis*, Trinity Term, 1922. Three poems: "In St. Simon's Memoirs," "Inscription in a copy of J. S. Mill's 'Principles of Political Economy,' " "Inscription in Rousseau's 'Contract Social.' " Unsigned, but in Waugh's scrapbook with his holograph emendations.

566 "Juvenalia," *Farrago* (Oxford), No. 2 (June 1930), 88.

567 "Stainless Stanley," *Spectator*, 198 (31 May 1957), 700.

6. Letters to the Editor

568 "In Defense of Cubism," *Drawing*, December 1917. See also response by G. E. d. M. in a subsequent issue. (These items are in Waugh's Scrapbook at the University of Texas.)

569 Letter to the Editor (about his making the Lancing College Debating Society a "closed" society), *Lancing College Magazine*, November 1921, pp. 82-83.

570 Answer to Letter of Lavernia Scargill, *Lancing College Magazine*, December 1921, p. 96.

571 "Rugger Night" (about brawling in London), *The Isis*, 7 February 1923, p. 8.

572 "D. G. Rossetti," *Times Literary Supplement*, 17 May 1928, p. 379.

573 Letter about *Tablet* attack on *A Handful of Dust* in column of William Hickey [Tom Driberg], *Daily Express*, 11 September 1934, p. 6.

574 "Edmund Campion," *Listener*, 15 (26 February 1936), 410-411.

575 "The Conquest of Abyssinia," *The Times*, 19 May 1936, p. 12.

576 "Latin--or Roman," *Tablet*, 180 (2 January 1937), 26.

577 "Christmas at Bethlehem," *Tablet*, 180 (9 January 1937), 62.

578 "Italian Reprisals in Addis Ababa," *The Times*, 12 March 1937, p. 17.

579 "Teresa Higginson," *Tablet*, 190 (11 December 1937), 803. Plea for precise investigation of stories of marvels.

580 "Fascist," *New Statesman and Nation*, 15 (5 March 1938), 365-366.

581 "Mrs. Evelyn Waugh's Review" (corrections for review of *Enemies of Promise*), *Tablet*, 181 (10 December 1938), 805.

582 "B.B.C. Bulletins," *The Times*, 20 February 1939, p. 8.

583 "Journey to a War," *Spectator*, 162 (21 April 1939), 674. An answer to Stephen Spender's objection to Waugh's review of *Journey to a War* [*Spectator*, 162 (24 March 1939)].

584 "In Defense of Mexico," *Spectator*, 162 (23 June 1939), 1095.

584a "Mr. Evelyn Waugh and the *Daily Mail*," *Tablet*, 182 (19 April 1939), 250.

585 [Excerpt from a letter to Cyril Connolly]. *Horizon*, 4 (November 1941), 299-302.

586 "Combatant," "Why Not War Writers?" *Horizon*, 4 (December 1941), 437-438. Unsigned, but included in a bound collection of articles by and about Waugh in the Waugh Collection at the University of Texas, and internal evidence links it closely with the language and tone of *Put Out More Flags*. The letter refers to "Why Not War Writers? A Manifesto," *Horizon*, 4 (October 1941), 236-239.

587 "Victorian Taste," *Times*, 3 March 1942, p. 5.

588 "Snobbery and Titles," *Spectator*, 168 (8 May 1942), 443.

589 Letter to the editor, *Horizon*, 7 (March 1943), 214. [Offering annual prize of £10 to be called "The Alfred Wallis Prize" for "the silliest contribution"]. Reply by Graham Greene, "Wallis and Waugh," *Horizon*, 7 (May 1943), 362. Suggests the prize bear Waugh's name.

590 "Religion in State Schools," letters to editor. *New Statesman and Nation*, 26 (2 October 1943), 217; (16 October 1943), 251.

591 "Picasso and Matisse," (in reply to letters from R. O. Dunlop and D. Saurat, "Picasso and Matisse," *Times*, 18 December 1945, p. 5), *Times*, 20 December 1945, p. 5.

592 "Foreign Travel for Young Writers," *Times*, 17 April 1947, p. 5.

593 "The Last Days of Hitler," *Tablet*, 189 (28 June 1947),
335.

594 "The Pieties of Evelyn Waugh," *The Bell*, 14 (July 1947),
77.

595 "A Visit to America," *Times*, 6 November 1947, p. 5.

596 "Evelyn Waugh Upholds Knox Version," *Universe*, 27
February 1948.

597 "Mr. Waugh on the Catholic Novelist," *Duckett's Register*,
March 1948.

598 "Christian Prayer," *Times*, 21 May 1948, p. 5.

599 "Christian Prayer," *Times*, 25 May 1948, p. 5.

600 "The Heart of the Matter," *Tablet*, 192 (17 July 1948), 41.

601 "Elected Silence," *New Statesman and Nation*, 38 (20
August 1949), 197; (3 September 1949), 245-246; (10
September 1949), 274; (17 December 1949), 302.

602 "Electric Sanctuary Lamps," *Tablet*, 196 (9 September
1950), 215.

603 "Matisse Builds a Church," *Tablet*, 196 (2 December 1950),
486.

604 "The South Bank at Night," with Christopher Sykes and
Douglas Woodruff, *Times*, 24 May 1951, p. 5.

605 "The Claque," *Sunday Times*, 12 August 1951, p. 8.

606 "Saint Helena," *Tablet*, 198 (3 November 1951), 324.

607 "Saint Helena," *Tablet*, 198 (17 November 1951), 364.

608 "Tax on Dollar Earnings," *Times*, 6 February 1952, p. 5.

609   "Taxation of Authors," *Times*, 24 May 1952, p. 7.

610   "Marshall Tito's Visit," *Spectator*, 189 (19 December 1952), 846.

611   "Tito and Stepinac," *New Statesman and Nation*, NS 45 (28 February 1953), 233.

612   "President Tito's Visit," *Times*, 24 March 1953, p. 9.

613   "Sir Thomas More," *New Statesman and Nation*, NS 46 (12 December 1953), 762. Response to H. R. Trevor-Roper's "Books in General," 5 December 1953, 735-736. Responses to this letter by Trevor-Roper and Sean O'Casey, 26 December 1953, 822.

614   "Sir Thomas More," *New Statesman and Nation*, NS 47 (2 January 1954), 16. Waugh's re-reply, followed by Trevor-Roper's, 9 January 1954, 41-42.

615   "Conditions in Goa," *Times*, 24 March 1954, p. 9.

616   "Hilaire Belloc," *New Statesman and Nation*, NS 48 (3 July 1954), 16. Response to review of Belloc's verse by James Reeves, 47 (26 June 1954), 838.

617   "Painter and Patron: Responsibilities to One Another," *Times*, 17 July 1954, p. 7.

618   "A Star for Silence," *Times*, 28 April 1955, p. 13.

618a "Graham Greene," *Catholic Herald*, 3 June 1955, p. 2.

619   "Stoner," *Tablet*, 206 (16 July 1955), 66. Letter also signed by Ronald Knox and Michael Trappes-Lomax.

620   "Statues in London," *Times*, 20 July 1955, p. 9.

621   "Men at Waugh," *Spectator*, 195 (22 July 1955), 121.

622   "P. G. Wodehouse," *Observer*, 12 February 1956, p. 12.

Reply to John Wain's review of *French Leave,* "New Novels," *Observer,* 29 January 1956, p. 9.

623   "Belloc Anadyomenos," *Spectator,* 195 (2 September 1955), 304.

624   "A Final View," *Four Quarters,* 5, No. 3 (March 1956), 18-19.

625   "Matisse Reliefs," *Times,* 20 June 1956, p. 11.

626   "A Poet of the Counter-Reformation," *Spectator,* 196 (13 July 1956), 63; (27 July 1956), 143.

627   "Deification and Clarification," *Spectator,* 196 (3 August 1956), 178; (10 August 1956), 206; (24 August 1956), 261.

628   "Popish Plotters," *New Statesman and Nation,* NS 52 (1 September 1956), 243. Response to Trevor-Roper's comment in "Books in General," 25 August 1956, 217. See reply by Trevor-Roper, 8 September 1956, 284.

628a   "Papist Plots," *New Statesman and Nation,* NS 52 (29 September 1956), 377. Trevor-Roper's reply, 6 October, p. 410.

629   "Mighty Old Artificer," *Spectator,* 196 (2 November 1956), 608.

630   "Monsignor Ronald Knox," *Tablet,* 210 (7 September 1957), 194.

631   "Mgr. R. A. Knox," *Tablet,* 211 (7 June 1958), 536. This letter is also signed by several others, e.g. C. S. Lewis and Harold Macmillan.

631a   "Mgr. Knox on St. Teresa," *Catholic Herald,* 11 July 1958, p. 2.

632   "An Unposted Letter," *Times,* 17 June 1959, p. 11.

633 "Social Distinctions," *Times*, 19 September 1959, p. 7.

634 "Mr. 'C,' " *New Statesman*, NS 58 (24 October 1959), 546. Response to Malcolm Muggeridge's comment in "London Diary," 17 October 1959, 499.

635 "The Life of Ronald Knox," *Tablet*, 213 (7 November 1959), 970.

636 "A Bishop's Rebuke," *Times*, 5 July 1960, p. 13.

637 "Lady Chatterley," *Spectator*, 205 (18 November 1960), 771.

638 "Evelyn Waugh Replies," *Encounter*, 15 (December 1960), 83. Reply to Frank Kermode's "Mr. Waugh's Cities," November 1960, 63-66, 68-70.

639 "Nihil Obstat," *Times*, 7 March 1961, p. 13.

640 "Old Men at the Zoo," *Spectator*, 207 (18 October 1961), 501. Reply to John Mortimer, "A Fatal Giraffe," *Spectator*, (29 September 1961), 431, a review of Angus Wilson, *Old Men at the Zoo.*

641 "Indexes," *Times*, 16 October 1961, p. 13.

642 "The Dialogue Mass," *Tablet*, 217 (16 March 1963), 292.

643 "The Council: Phase One," *Tablet*, 217 (7 September 1963), 969.

644 "The Council: Phase One," *Tablet*, 217 (21 September 1963), 1017.

645 "What is Expendable?" *Tablet*, 217 (28 September 1963), 1044.

646 "Changes in the Church," *Catholic Herald*, 7 August 1964, p. 4. This letter drew several replies in the August 14 issue of the *Herald*. One letter was entitled, "Waugh

the ex-Beatle,'' p. 5.

647 "Understanding the Conservatives,'' *Commonweal*, 80
(7 August 1964), 547-548. Response to John Cogley,
"Understanding the Conservatives,'' 19 June 1964,
pp. 388-389, and to ''The Council and Anti-Semitism,''
26 June 1964, pp. 407-408. And see William Kupersmith's reply to Waugh, 21 August 1964, pp. 580-581.

648 "Using English in the Latin Mass,'' *Times*, 8 August
1964, p. 7. Reply to letter from Edward Hutton, ''Using
English in the Latin Mass,'' *Times*, 6 August 1964, p. 9.

649 "Changes in the Church,'' *Catholic Herald*, 7 August 1964,
p. 4. Replies, 13 August, p. 5; 21 August, p. 5.

650 "A Suggestion for Mr. Waugh,'' *Commonweal*, 81 (4 December 1964), 352-353.

651 "An Aid to Participation?'' *Tablet*, 219 (24 April 1965),
473.

652 "Fides Quaerens Intellectum,'' *Tablet*, 219 (31 July 1965),
864.

653 "Edwardian Life,'' *Spectator*, 215 (6 August 1965), 176.

654 "Sweetness of Temper,'' *Tablet*, 219 (14 August 1965), 914 .

655 "Fides Quaerens Intellectum,'' *Tablet*, 219 (21 August
1965), 938.

656 "Some Modest Proposals from Illinois,'' *Tablet*, 219 (18
September 1965), 1040.

657 "A Post-Waugh Insight,'' *Commonweal*, 83 (7 January 1966),
391. Reply to J. M. Cameron's article.

D. Interviews

Entries are arranged chronologically, except for reprinted material, which is listed under the first appearance.

658   Black, Stephen, interviewer, "Personal Call, No. 14."
      London: BBC radio, 29 September 1953. Unpublished.

659   Black, Stephen, Jack Davies and Charles Wilmot, inter-
      viewers, "Frankly Speaking." London: BBC radio,
      16 November 1953. Unpublished.

660   Ryan, T.C., "A Talk With Evelyn Waugh," *Sign*, 37 (Au-
      gust 1957), 41-43.

661   Freeman, John, interviewer, "Face to Face." London:
      BBC TV, 26 June 1960. Unpublished. See the two
      following items.

662   Crozier, Mary, "Interviewing Mr. Waugh," *Tablet*, 214 (2
      July 1960), 623. A brief account of Waugh being inter-
      viewed on "Face to Face" program.

663   *Face to Face*, ed. Hugh Burnett. London: Jonathan Cape,
      1964. Pp. 94-95. Contains a comment uttered by Waugh
      on the "Face to Face" interview.

664   (Interview with Julian Jebb) "The Art of Fiction XXX:
      Evelyn Waugh," *Paris Review* 8 (Summer-Fall 1963),
      72-85. Reprinted in *Writers at Work. The Paris Re-
      view Interviews*, Third Series (New York: Viking, 1967),
      pp. 103-114.

664a Allsop, Kenneth. "Pinfold at Home," *Scan*. London:
      Hodder and Stoughton, 1965. Pp. 98-101.

665   Jebb, Julian, "Evelyn Waugh: Facing the Inquisition," [Lon-
      don] *Times Saturday Review*, 23 December 1967, p. 9.
      The *Paris Review* material with some additional anec-
      dotes.

E. Broadcasts.

666   "To an Unnamed Listner. No. VII. To an Old Man,"
       28 November 1932, Daventry National, Monday,
       9:20 p.m. Unpublished.

667   "Sale-Room Entertainment," *Listener*, 19 (2 June 1938),
       1168. Excerpt from a broadcast, West, 20 May 1938.

F. Remarks

This rather unusual category is necessary because Waugh's
comments were regarded as good copy and were not only reported
but solicited. The items are arranged chronologically by date of
publication.

668   Statement about the "travel book" in "Determined--To
       Impress," by Lady Eleanor Smith, "From a Window in
       Vanity Fair," *Sunday Dispatch*, 3 February 1929, p. 4.

669   Remarks in Benefit Programme at Oxford. Reported by "Mr.
       Gossip," "Preservation of Oxford--Evelyn Waugh Sug-
       gests Dynamite," *Daily Sketch*, 23 February 1930, p. 5.

670   On J. Keith Winter, *Other Man's Saucer*, in Heinemann ad-
       vertisement of June 1930.

671   On Louis Marlow, *The Lion Took Fright*, in Mundanus (Gol-
       lancz) advertisement of October 1930.

672   About Lady Longford [Christine Trew], *Making Conversa-
       tion*, quoted in advertisement of Leonard Stein(Gollancz),
       The Observer, 1 November 1931, p. 7.

673   On his favorite book in Cecil Hunt, *Author-Biography.*
      London: Hutchinson, 1935. P. 216. Remark made
      c. 1933.

674   Remarks on Laurence Oliver, *Tadpoles and God,* quoted
      in *The Cherwell,* 28 April 1934, p. 20.

675   To William Hickey about Peter Fleming's ruining the
      sales of travel books, *The Daily Express,* 3 September
      1934, p. 6. Letter.

676   To William Hickey [Tom Driberg] about *The Tablet's*
      attack on *A Handful of Dust, The Daily Express,* 11
      September 1934, p. 6.

677   Remark in 1934 about divorce, in Doris Langley Moore,
      *The Vulgar Heart, An Inquiry into the Sentimental
      Tendencies of Public Opinion.* London: Cassell,
      1945. P. 103.

678   "Italy in Abyssinia" delivered on 7 June 1936, before the
      Newman Society, Oxford. Reported in *The Cherwell,*
      13 June 1936, p. 164; *Tablet,* 13 June 1936, pp. 750-
      751.

679   "Ideological Writing" delivered at *The Sunday Times Book
      Fair,* 12 November 1937, reported in *Sunday Times,* 14
      November 1937, p. 31.

680   "The History and Associations of Woodchester Park," a
      paper read at Dursley on Whit Monday to open the cam-
      paign for building the Dursley Catholic Church. Repor-
      ted in "Town and Country," *Tablet,* 18 June 1938,
      p. 815.

681   Supporting Douglas Woodruff's Toast at the Farewell Din-
      ner for Msgr. Ronald Knox at Oxford. Reported in
      "Oxford's Farewell to Mgr. Knox," *Tablet,* 17 June
      1939, p. 790.

682   "Warning" ["carried on the inside cover" of the English

edition of *Brideshead Revisited*] in Harold Gardner, "Follow up on Waugh," *America*, 74 (16 February 1946), 536.

683 "Waugh Lecture; Noted British Wit Discusses Three Fellow Convert Writers, Chesterton, Knox, and Greene," *Books on Trial*, 7 (April 1949), 277, 301.

684 [Some of Waugh's remarks in a speech to the Newman Society at Derby, England], *Books on Trial*, 10 (April 1952), 293.

685 [Excerpt from a letter to Anne Ford], *Harbrace Folio*, No. 9, October 1953, p. 2.

686 [Comments on merits of modern film and novel] in *Film en Roman*. Amsterdam: De Kim, 1956. P. 16.

687 "Books of the Year II," *Sunday Times*, 1 January 1956, p. 7. A brief comment by Waugh on the best books written during 1955.

688 A note from Waugh about writing the life of Knox, *The Critic*, October 1957, p. 48.

G. Debates

689 "The Doctrine of Re-incarnation offers the best Solution to the Problem of Immortality," as the Proposer, *Lancing College Magazine*, December 1919, p. 106.

690 "This Group Approves the Government's Bill for the Reconstruction of the Public Schools," as the Proposer, before the Debate Group of the Dilettanti Society, Lancing College, reported in "The Dilettanti," *Lancing College Magazine*, March 1920, pp. 7-8.

691 "The Bachelor is better off than the Paterfamilas," on Pro side as seventh speaker, reported in *Lancing College Magazine*, April 1920, pp. 18-20.

692 "Curiosity is the best Trait in the Character of Most Human Beings," on Con side as eighth speaker, reported in *Lancing College Magazine*, June 1920, pp. 39-40.

693 "This House Deplores the Disrespect shown by the Youth of Today to its Elders," as Opposer, reported in *Lancing College Magazine*, November 1920, p. 81.

694 "Man's One and Only Object is his Pleasure," on Pro side as sixth speaker, reported in *Lancing College Magazine*, December 1920, p. 102.

695 "Smoking Should be Made Compulsory for the Young," as Opposer, reported in *Lancing College Magazine*, February 1921, pp. 5-6.

696 "Science is the Root of all Evil," on Pro side as fourth speaker, reported in *Lancing College Magazine*, March 1921, p. 20.

697 "This House Would Welcome Abolition of the House of Commons," as Proposer, reported in *Lancing College Magazine*, June 1921, p. 39.

698 "The Rejection of Dominion Home Rule is in the Interests of the Irish Nation," as President, reported in *Lancing College Magazine*, November 1921, p. 76.

699 "The Canons of Good Taste Rather Than the Laws of Morality are Outraged by Murder," as fourth speaker, reported in *Lancing College Magazine*, November 1921, p. 76.

700 "This House Considers that the Day of Institutional Religion is Over," on Con side, reported in *Lancing College Magazine*, December 1921, p. 91.

701   "This House deplores the Invention of the Cinema," as
        Opposer, reported in *Lancing College Magazine*, December 1921, p. 92.

702   "This House Would Welcome Prohibition," a "maiden
        speech." Reported in *The Isis*, 8 February 1922, p.
        12; *The Oxford Magazine*, 23 February 1922, p. 246.

704   "The Future of Industry depends upon Private Enterprise,"
        on Pro side. Reported in *The Cherwell*, 21 February
        1922, p. 76; *The Isis*, 22 February 1922, p. 6; *The
        Oxford Magazine*, 23 February 1922, p. 246.

706   "The Government Should Adopt at Once a Foreign Policy
        based on the League of Nations," on Con side. Reported in *The Isis*, 24 May 1922, p. 26; *The Cherwell*,
        25 May 1922, p. 44; *The Oxford Magazine*, 25 May
        1922, pp. 384-385.

707   "This House Deplores the Tendencies of Modern Democracy," on Pro side. Reported in *The Isis*, 7 June
        1922, p. 2; *The Cherwell*, 8 June 1922, pp. 79-80;
        The Oxford Magazine, 8 June 1922, pp. 419-420.

708   "The Introduction of Prohibition would Benefit this Country,"
        on Pro side. Reported in *The Isis*, 29 November 1922,
        p. 15; *The Oxford Magazine*, 30 November 1922, p. 123.

709   "This House deplores present French Policy as a Menace
        to Europe," as Neutral speaker. Reported in *The Isis*,
        31 January 1923, p. xviii; *The Oxford Magazine*, 1
        February 1923, p. 181.

710   "The Time is come to bury the Hatchet with the Central
        Powers," on Con side. Reported in *The Isis*, 28
        February 1923, p. 4; *The Oxford Magazine*, 1 March
        1923, pp. 258-259.

711   "This House places full Confidence in His Majesty's
        Government," as fifth speaker. Reported in *The Isis*,
        13 June 1923, p. 13; no account of actual speech.

712 "Reform of the Divorce Laws along the lines of Lord
Buckmaster's Proposals," on Con side. Reported in
The Isis, 7 November 1923, p. 14; *The Oxford Magazine*,
8 November 1923, p. 87; *The Cherwell*, 10 November
1923, p. 51.

713 "Regret that the Population of England has gone over
Five Millions," on Pro side. Reported in *The Isis*,
14 November 1923, p. 13; *The Oxford Magazine*, 15
November 1923, pp. 110-111; *The Cherwell*, 17 November 1923, pp. 75-76.

714 "Private Business" motion to raise dues. Reported in
The Isis, 30 January 1924, p. 15; *The Cherwell*, 2
February 1924, p. 58.

715 "That This House Approves the Support Given by France
to the Separatists in the Ruhr," as opposer of evidence.
Reported in *The Isis*, 6 February 1924, p. 13; *The Oxford Magazine*, 7 February 1924, pp. 252-254; *The Cherwell*, 9 February 1924, p. 54.

715a "That Shakespeare did not Intend Hamlet to be Mad," on
Pro side. Reported in *The Isis*, 20 February 1924,
p. 19; *The Oxford Magazine*, 21 February 1924, p. 302;
The Cherwell, 23 February 1924, pp. 115-116.

715b "That Immediate and Drastic Reform is needed in our so-
called Public Schools," on Pro side. Reported in
The Cherwell, 17 May 1924, p. 69; *The Isis*, 22 May
1924, p. 34; *The Oxford Magazine*, 22 May 1924, pp.
474-475.

716 Proposing the Abolition of the Press at the Oxford Union
Society. Reported in "The Union," *The Cherwell*, 27
May 1939, p. 91.

H. Drawings, Bookplates, and Dust-Jacket Designs.

The entries in this category are listed chronologically, except for the undatable bookplates, which are listed at the end.

717 With Hooper Minor. "Heath Mount BC 55," *The Cynic*, 8 February 1916, p. 2.

718 Dust-jacket design for *A Pair of Idols*, by Stewart Caven. London: Chapman and Hall, 1919.

719 Dust-jacket design for *Invisible Tides*, by Beatrice Kean Seymour. London: Chapman and Hall, 1919.

720 "The Rag Regatta," *Isis*, 14 June 1922, p. 9. Signed "Scaramel."

721 "Men Who Talk Too Much," *The Isis*, 14 June 1922, p. 18. Cartoon.

722 "Heard at the College Debating Society," *The Isis*, 18 October 1922, p. 7.

723 "An Impression of the Union Library, A.D., 1922," *The Isis*, 18 October 1922, p. 20.

724 "The Great Club Problem," *The Isis*, 25 October 1922, p. 10.

725 "Evolution and Plus Fours," *The Isis*, 1 November 1922, p. 10.

726 Book-plate for Richard Pares (1922).

727 "Suggestions for Alley Workshops Toy: Mr. Pares, Editor of *The New Oxford*," *Isis*, 24 January 1923, p. 7.

728   Cover Cartoon (a sweeper), *The Oxford Broom*, April 1923.

729   "The Union" (a column-head cartoon of speaker in the
      Union), *The Isis*, 9 May 1923, p. 11, and weekly after-
      ward.

730   "Bertram, Ludovic, and Ann" (three insects over a boy's
      bed) for "The Children's Corner," *The Isis*, 24 May
      1923, p. 23.

731   Bookplates. Shown at the Oxford Arts Club Exhibition in
      June 1923, Oxford University. Reported by Arundel
      del Re, "Oxford Arts Club," *The Isis*, 20 June 1923,
      p. 12.

732   Cover Cartoon (a unicorn and a sweeper), *The Oxford
      Broom*, June 1923.

733   Cover Cartoon and Editorial Page Cartoon (of "the Oxford
      stage"), *The Cherwell*, 1 August 1923, and weekly
      afterward until 1929.

734   "Book Reviews" (a column-head cartoon of readers and a
      bookpile), *The Cherwell*, 15 August 1923, p. 59,
      and weekly afterward.

735   "The Seven Deadly Sins. No. I. The Intolerable Wicked-
      ness of Him Who Drinks Alone," *The Cherwell*, 17
      October 1923, p. 238.

736   "The Seven Deadly Sins. No. II. The Horrid Sacrilege
      of those that Ill-treat Books," *The Cherwell*, 27
      October 1923, p. 14.

737   "Youth," *The London Mercury*, 8 (October 1923), 635.

738   "The Seven Deadly Sins. No. III. The Wanton Way of
      those that corrupt the very young," *The Cherwell*, 3
      November 1923, p. 32.

739   "The Union" (a column-head cartoom of speaker and

foreign listeners), *The Cherwell*, 10 November 1923, p. 51, and weekly afterward.

740 ''The Oxford Playhouse'' (a column-head cartoon of a clown), *The Cherwell*, 10 November 1923, p. 56, and weekly afterward.

741 ''The Seven Deadly Sins. No. IV. The Hideous Habit of Marrying Negroes,'' *The Cherwell*, 10 November 1923, p. 64.

742 ''The Seven Deadly Sins. No. V. That Grim Act Parricide,'' *The Cherwell*, 17 November 1923, p. 77.

743 ''London Letter'' (a column-head cartoon), *The Isis*, Fall Term, 1923, used several times.

744 ''The Seven Deadly Sins. No. VI. That dull, old Sin Adultery,'' *The Cherwell*, 24 November 1923, p. 110.

745 ''The Seven Deadly Sins. No. VII. The Grave Discourtesy of such a man as will beat his host's servant,'' *The Cherwell*, 24 November 1923, p. 116.

746 ''Paris Letter'' (a column-head cartoon of a street scene in France), *The Isis*, 28 November 1923, p. 13, and weekly for several issues.

747 ''New Theatre'' (a column-head cartoon of Stage, crew Author, and Actors), *The Isis*, 28 November 1923, p. 21, and weekly afterward for the twenties and part of the thirties.

748 Dust-jacket design for *Grass of Parnassus*, by Mary Fulton. London: Chapman and Hall, 1923.

749 Dust-jacket design for *Clent's Way*, by C. C. and E. M. Molt. London: Chapman and Hall, 1923.

750 Dust-jacket design for *Colleagues*, by Geraldine Waife. London: Chapman and Hall, 1923.

751 Dust-jacket design for *Circular Saws*, by Humbert Wolfe. London: Chapman and Hall, 1923.

752 "Angostura and Soda," *The Isis*, 30 January 1924, p. 5.

753 Drawings in *The Golden Hind*, 2, No. 6 (January 1924), 26, 39, 43.

754 "Cornish Landscape with White Cow in Thought," *The Cherwell*, 2 February 1924, p. 40.

755 Cover Cartoon (of a merry-go-round of Unicorns and Sweepers mounted), *The Oxford Broom*, in *The Cherwell*, 9 February 1924, p. 63.

756 "Brandy," *The Isis*, 12 March 1924, p. 10.

757 "Beer," *The Isis*, 7 May 1924, p. 4.

758 "The Tragical Death of Mr. Will. Huskisson. September MDCCCXXX," *The Cherwell*, 24 May 1924, pp. 86-87. Also exhibited at the Oxford Arts Club Exhibition, June 1924; reported in *The Isis*, 18 June 1924, pp. 18-19; *The Oxford Chronicle*, 20 June 1924, p. 16.

759 Dust-jacket for *Kittens Tale*, by Jane Burr. London: Cecil Palmer, 1924.

760 Dust-jacket for *The Scrap Heap*, by Geraldine Waife, London: Chapman and Hall, 1924.

761 Dust-jacket design for *Card Castle*, by Alec Waugh. London: Grant Richards, 1924.

762 Book-plate for Dudley Carew. 1924.

763 Book-plate for Arthur Waugh. 1924.

764 "Music" (a column-head cartoon of a woman singing), *The Cherwell*, 7 November 1924, p. 93, and after for several issues.

768 Drawing for Christmas card, 1927.

766 Dust-jacket design for *Children of the Peace*, by Barbara Goolden. London: Chapman and Hall, 1928.

767 Dust-jacket design for *The Old Expedient*, by Pansy Pakenham. London: Chapman and Hall, 1928.

768 Dust Wrapper Cartoon and six illustrations for *Decline and Fall, an illustrated Novelette.* London: Chapman and Hall, 1928. The hero is depicted in four types of dress with unchanged countenance, reported by "Dragoman," in "The Talk of London," *Daily Express*, 18 September 1928, p. 19.

769 Cover and Editorial Page Cartoon (revised and modernized), *The Cherwell*, 2 February 1929, and weekly afterward until 1940.

770 Dust Wrapper Cartoon (of Edwardian street scene) for *Three Score and Ten*, by Alec Waugh. London: Chapman and Hall, 1929.

771 Christmas Card for 1929 (made of newspaper headlines in "Futurist" design). Reported by Dragoman, "The Talk of London," *Daily Express*, 24 December 1930, p. 9.

772 Dust Wrapper Cartoon (used also as Frontispiece) for *Vile Bodies*, 17 January 1930.

773 Dust Wrapper Cartoon for *Labels, A Mediterranean Journal*, 19 October 1930. Photograph in *Bystander*, 1 October 1930, p. 48.

774 Illustrations for *Black Mischief*. London: Chapman and Hall, 1932. (1 October).

775 Pastiches for illustrations of *Love Among the Ruins*. London: Chapman and Hall, 1953.

776 Illustrations for *Decline and Fall, Art News,* 54 (December 1955), 26.

777 Book-plate for R. T. B. Fulford.

778 Book-plate for John Greenidge.

779 Book-plate for D. J. V. Hamilton Miller.

780 Book-plate for Alexander Raban Waugh.

I. Editor and Staff Member

781 Editor of *The Pistol Troop Magazine.* Underhill: At the Pistol Troop Press, 1912.

782 Editor of *The Cynic,* a mimeographed magazine distributed at Heath Mount School. Five issues, 21 January 1916; 8 February 1916; 7 March 1916; 5 May 1916; September 1916.

783 Editor of *Lancing College Magazine,* November, December 1921.

784 Business Manager and Editor of *The Oxford Fortnightly Review, a Political, Social and Literary Journal.* Published under the auspices of the Oxford Carlton Club. Issues of 21 October 1922; 4 November 1922; 18 November 1922; 2 December 1922.

785 *The Oxford Broom,* as "Editor's support" and contributor to the four numbers of February, April, and June 1923, and the last delayed number which was published with *The Cherwell,* 9 February 1924, pp. 63-ff.

786   *The Isis* (with which is encorporated *The Varsity: A Social View of Oxford Life*), as "Union" reporter in Summer Term, 1923, and "Cinema" reviewer in Fall Term, 1923.

787   Sub-editor of *The Isis*, Spring Term, 1924; the eight numbers from January 23 to March 12.

J. Miscellaneous

788   Description and reproduction of p. 1 of the manuscript of *Rossetti: His Life and Work, Catalogue of Nineteenth Century and Modern First Editions, Presentation Copies, Autograph Letters and Important Literary Manuscripts.* London: Sotheby, 12 December 1961.

789   "Bruno Hatte" (a hoaxing advertisement of an exhibition of paintings, done with Brian Howard). Reported by Lady Eleanor Smith, "From a Window in Vanity Fair," *Sunday Dispatch*, 14 July 1929, p. 4; quoted by Patrick Balfour, *Society Racket, a Critical Survey of Modern Social Life.* London: John Long, 1932.

790   *Vile Bodies, a Play in Twelve Episodes.* Adapted by H. Dennis Bradley, London: Chapman and Hall, 1931. Twelve performances at the Arts Theatre Club, October 1931. Reviewed in *G. K's Weekly*, 15 (14 May 1932), 375.

791   "The Man Who Liked Dickens," a Television Play Adapted by Robert Tallman, *Literary Cavalcade* (April 1954). Readily accessible in *Adventures in Appreciation*, ed. Walter Loban, Dorothy Holmstrom, Luella B. Cook (New York: Harcourt, Brace, 1958), pp. 432-447.

791a *Evelyn Waugh Reading from His Works* [*Vile Bodies* and *Helena*]. Verve 12 inch record, MG 1508. Recorded 9 April 1960.

792   Montgomery, John. *The Fifties.* London: Allen and Unwin, 1965. Quotations and paraphrase of 1960 *Daily Mail* article by Waugh, pp. 361-362.

792a Southern, Terry. *The Journal of The Loved One: The Production Log of a Motion Picture.* New York: Random House, 1965.

792b *Evelyn Waugh's Decline and Fall adapted for the screen by Ivan Foxwell.* Additional scenes by Alan Hackney and Hugh Whitemore. London: Supotype Ltd., [1965].

793   "Waugh on Waugh," *Sunday Telegraph,* 17 April 1966. Contains excerpts from various prefaces to several of the New Uniform Editions.

794   "Film Clips: The Scarlet Woman," *Sight and Sound,* 36, No. 3 (Summer 1967), 154-155.

795   "The Scarlet Woman," *Evelyn Waugh Newsletter,* 3 (Autumn 1969), 1-7. Edited by Charles E. Linck under the title "Waugh-Greenidge Film--*The Scarlet Woman.*"

PART II: WORKS ABOUT EVELYN WAUGH

This part is divided into five sections: Bibliographies, Books and Monographs, Dissertations, Articles on General Topics, and Articles and Reviews on Individual Works. The basic arrangement is alphabetical; however, the final section lists, first, critical articles for each book, then reviews of that book. Reviewers are listed alphabetically; anonymous reviews or those for which the index gave no reviewer are listed alphabetically by journal title.

A. Bibliographies

796 Bogaards, Winnifred M. "Waugh's Letters to *The Times*," *Evelyn Waugh Newsletter*, 3 (Winter 1969), 5-6.

797 Davis, Robert Murray. "Some Unidentified Works by Evelyn Waugh," *Evelyn Waugh Newsletter*, 4 (Winter 1970), 6-7.

798 Doyle, Paul A. "Evelyn Waugh: A Bibliography (1926 - 1956)," *Bulletin of Bibliography*, 22 (May-August 1957), 57-62.

799 --- "Waugh Correspondence in the Fales Collection, NYU," *Evelyn Waugh Newsletter*, 3 (Autumn 1969), 7-9.

800 --- "Evelyn's Letters at Boston University," *Evelyn Waugh Newsletter*, 4 (Winter 1970), 5-6.

801 --- "Some Unpublished Waugh Correspondence III," *Evelyn Waugh Newsletter*, 5 (Spring 1971), 3-4.

802 --- and Charles E. Linck. "Some Unpublished Waugh Correspondence," *Evelyn Waugh Newsletter*, 2 (Spring 1968), 6; 2 (Winter 1968), 3-4.

803 --- , Winnifred Bogaards, and Robert M. Davis. "Works of Waugh 1940-1966: A Supplementary Bibliography, Part I," *Evelyn Waugh Newsletter*, 4 (Winter 1970), 7-10; "Part 2", *Evelyn Waugh Newsletter*, 5 (Spring 1971), 8-13.

804 English, William A. "Some Irish and English Waugh Bibliography," *Evelyn Waugh Newsletter*, 1 (Winter 1967), 5; 2 (Autumn 1968), 3-4.

805 Farr, D. Paul. "Evelyn Waugh: A Supplemental Bibliography," *Bulletin of Bibliography*, 26 (July-September 1969), 67-68, 87.

806 Gallagher, D. S. "Towards a Definitive Waugh Bibliography: Notations on the 1957 *BB* Checklist," *Evelyn Waugh Newsletter*, 5 (Spring 1971), 6-8.

807 --- "Additional Waugh Bibliography," *Evelyn Waugh Newsletter*, 5 (Autumn 1971), 6-7.

808 Kosok, Heinz. "Evelyn Waugh: A Checklist of Criticism," *Twentieth Century Literature*, 11 (1965-1966), 211-215.

809 --- "Evelyn Waugh: A Supplementary Checklist of Criticism," *Evelyn Waugh Newsletter*, 2 (Spring 1968), 1-3; 3 (Spring 1969), 4-5; 4 (Spring 1970), 6-8; 5 (Spring 1971), 4-5.

810 LaFrance, Marston. "Charles E. Linck's Bibliography of Waugh's Early Work, 1910-1930; Some Additions and Corrections," *Evelyn Waugh Newsletter*, 4 (Autumn 1970), 8-9.

811 Linck, Charles E. "Bibliography: Works of Evelyn Waugh, 1910-1940," *The Development of Evelyn Waugh's Career: 1903-1939*, pp. 343-390 (doctoral dissertation available through University Microfilms, Ann Arbor, Michigan, in book facsimile or microfilm form).

812 --- "Works of Evelyn Waugh, 1910-1930," *Twentieth Century Literature*, 10 (April 1964), 19-26.

813 --- "Waugh Letters at the Texas Academic Center," *Evelyn Waugh Newsletter*, 1 (Winter 1967), 1-5.

814 --- "A Waugh Letter Postmarked Chicago," *Evelyn Waugh Newsletter*, 4 (Spring 1970), 8.

815 Tosser, Yvon. "Bibliography of Waugh Criticism (French Area): Part I," *Evelyn Waugh Newsletter*, 4 (Spring 1970), 8-9.

B. Books and Monographs

816 Bradbury, Malcolm. *Evelyn Waugh*. Writers and Critics Series. Edinburgh: Oliver and Boyd, 1964.
Reviews:
Davis, R. M. *Modern Language Journal*, 51 (February 1967), 115.
Whittingten-Egan, R. *Books and Bookmen*, 10 (January 1965), 34.
Times Literary Supplement, 17 December 1964, p. 1146.

817 Carens, James F. *The Satiric Art of Evelyn Waugh.* Seattle and London: University of Washington Press, 1966.
Reviews:
Allen, G. W. *Saturday Review*, 49 (11 June 1966), 64.
Benstock, Bernard. *Southern Review*, Summer 1968, p. 802.
Cayton, R. F. *Library Journal*, 91 (July 1966), 3429.
Davis, R. M. *Modern Language Journal*, 51 (February 1967), 115.
Kosok, Heinz. *Die Neuren Sprachen*, 18 (1969), 634.

Nichols, James W. *Satire Newsletter*, 4 (1967), 102-104.

Robinson, J. K. *Books Today*, 3 (15 May 1966), 3.

Theall, B. *America*, 114 (21 May 1966), 745.

Wiley, P. L. *Contemporary Literature*, 11 (Spring 1968), 261-264.

Choice, 3 (October 1966), 634.

Times Literary Supplement, 24 August 1967, p. 759.

818 Cook, William J., Jr. *Masks, Modes, and Morals: The Art of Evelyn Waugh.* Cranbury, N. J.: Fairleigh Dickinson University Press, 1971.

819 Davis, Robert Murray (ed.). *Evelyn Waugh.* The Christian Critics Series. St. Louis: B. Herder, 1969.
Review:
James F. Carens, *Evelyn Waugh Newsletter*, 4 (Spring 1970), 9.

820 De Vitis, A. A. *Roman Holiday: The Catholic Novels of Evelyn Waugh.* New York: Bookman Associates, 1956; London, 1958.

821 Donaldson, Frances. *Evelyn Waugh: Portrait of a Country Neighbour.* London: Weidenfeld and Nicholson, 1967; Philadelphia: Chilton Books, 1968.
Reviews:
Braybrooke, Neville. *Spectator*, 12 May 1967, pp. 557-558.
Carens, James F. *Evelyn Waugh Newsletter*, 1 (Winter 1967), 6-7.
Shrapnel, Norman. *Manchester Guardian*, 12 May 1967.
Toynbee, Philip. *Observer*, 14 May 1967.
White, Terence De Vere. *Irish Times*, 13 May 1967.
Earl of Wicklow. *Hibernia*, June 1967.
Times Literary Supplement, 24 August 1967, p. 759.

822 Doyle, Paul A. *Evelyn Waugh*, Contemporary Writers in Christian Perspective Series (Grand Rapids, Michigan: Eerdmans, 1969).

Review:
Charles E. Linck, Jr. *Evelyn Waugh Newsletter,*
3 (Winter 1969), 6-8.

823 Greenblatt, Stephen Jay. *Three Modern Satirists: Waugh,*
Orwell, and Huxley. (New Haven: Yale University
Press, 1965).
Review:
Robert Murray Davis, *Books Abroad,* January 1967.

824 Hollis, Christopher. *Evelyn Waugh,* Writers and Their Work
No. 46. London: Longmans, Green, 1954. Revised
edition, 1958.

824a Schluter, Kurt. *Kuriose Welt im modernen englischen Roman:*
Dargestellt an auswählten Werken von Evelyn Waugh
und Angus Wilson. Berlin: Erich Schmidt, 1969.
Reviews:
Schafer, Jurgen. *Praxis des neusprachlichen*
Unterrichts, 17 (1970), 318-319.
Tomkins, J. M. S. *Studia Neophilologica,* 42 (1970),
480-481.

825 Stopp, Frederick J. *Evelyn Waugh, Portrait of an Artist.*
London: Chapman and Hall, 1958; Boston: Little, Brown
and Company, 1958.
Reviews:
Corbishley, T. *Month,* NS 20 (December 1958), 365-
367. See Stopp's reply, *Month,* NS 21 (March 1959),
196-198.
Elmen, Paul. *Christian Century,* 76 (14 October 1959),
1194.
Engle, Paul. *Chicago Sunday Tribune,* 18 January
1959, p. 5.
Fulford, Roger. *Time and Tide,* 39 (15 November
1958), 1373-1374.
Kennebeck, Edwin. *Commonweal,* 70 (24 April 1959),
110.
Kilcoyne, F. P. *Catholic World,* 189 (July 1959), 332.
McLaughlin, Richard. *Springfield Republican,* 22 March
1959, p. 4.

Martin, Jean. *Nation,* 188 (7 February 1959), 124.

Muggeridge, Malcolm. *New Republic,* 140 (26 January 1959), 18.

Miller, Kenneth. *San Francisco Chronicle,* 15 February 1959, p. 26.

O'Connor, W. V. *Saturday Review,* 42 (31 January 1959), 16.

Raven, Simon. *Spectator,* 31 October 1958, p. 588.

Wermuth, P. C. *Library Journal,* 84 (1 January 1959), 96.

Booklist, 55 (15 February 1959), 310.

Bookmark, 18 (January 1959), 94.

Kirkus, 26 (1 November 1958), 838.

New Yorker, 34 (17 January 1959), 97.

Times, 18 December 1958, p. 13.

Times Literary Supplement, 19 December 1958, p. 736.

826 Waugh, Alec. *My Brother Evelyn & Other Profiles.* London: Cassell, 1967; New York: Farrar, Straus and Giroux, 1967. Pp. 162-198. Revised version of *Atlantic* article.
Reviews:
Connolly, Cyril. *Sunday Times,* 22 October 1967, p. 55.
Davis, Robert M. *Evelyn Waugh Newsletter,* 2 (Spring 1968), 6-8.
Gawin, John. *Irish Press,* 28 October 1967, p. 6.
Lord Kinross (Patrick Balfour). *Envoy* (London), November 1967.
Sykes, Christopher. *Listener,* 78 (1967), 533.
Wall, Mervyn. *Hibernia* (Dublin), November 1967, p. 25 .

C. Dissertations

827 Bogaards, Winnifred M. "Ideas and Values in the Work of Evelyn Waugh." University of Saskatchewan, 1969.

828   Brennan, Neil Francis. "The Aesthetic Tradition in the
       English Comic Novel." University of Illinois, 1959.
       See *Dissertation Abstracts*, 20, No. 5 (1959), 1780-
       1781.

829   Carens, James F. "Evelyn Waugh: His Satire, His Ideas
       of Order, and His Relation to Other Modern English
       Satirical Novelists." Columbia University, 1959.
       Summary: *Dissertation Abstracts*, 20 (1959), 1362.

830   Cook, William J. "The Personae Technique of Evelyn
       Waugh." Auburn University, 1968. See *Dissertation
       Abstracts*, 29, No. 8, Series A. (1969), 2704-2705.

830a   Churchill, Thomas. "The House of Waugh: A Critical
       Study of Evelyn Waugh's Major Novels." University
       of Washington, 1964. Summary: *Dissertation Abstracts*,
       24 (1964), 2906.

831   Davis, Robert Murray. "The Externalist Method in The
       Novels of Ronald Firbank, Carl Van Vechten, and
       Evelyn Waugh." University of Wisconsin, 1964. See
       Dissertation Abstracts, 25, No. 4 (1964), 2509.

832   Dauch, Alfred. "Das Menschenbild in den Werken Evelyn
       Waughs." University of Cologne, 1955.

833   De Vitis, A. A. "The Religious Theme in the Novels of
       Rex Warner, Evelyn Waugh, and Graham Greene."
       University of Wisconsin, 1954. Summary: *University
       of Wisconsin Summaries of Doctoral Dissertations*, 15
       (1955), 605-606.

834   Dooley, D. J. "The Impact of Satire on Fiction: Studies
       in Norman Douglas, Sinclair Lewis, Aldous Huxley,
       Evelyn Waugh, and George Orwell." State University
       of Iowa, 1955. Summary: *Dissertation Abstracts*, 15
       (1955), 2203-2204.

835   Duer, Harriet Whitney. "All us Exiles: The Novels of
       Evelyn Waugh." University of Connecticut, 1970.

Summary: *Dissertation Abstracts*, 31, Series A (September 1970), 1269.

836   Jervis, Steven Alexander. "The Novels of Evelyn Waugh: A Critical Study." Stanford University, 1966. Summary: *Dissertation Abstracts*, 27 (1966), 1058A.

837   Linck, Charles Edward. "The Development of Evelyn Waugh's Career: 1903-1939." University of Kansas, 1962. Summary: *Dissertation Abstracts*, 24 (1963), 747-748.

838   McCay, Robert D. "Idea and Pattern in the Novels of Evelyn Waugh." State University of Iowa, 1952. Summary: *Dissertation Abstracts*, 13 (1953), 1197.

839   Skerle, Liselotte. "Das Wesen der Satire Evelyn Waughs." University of Graz, 1954.

840   Wallis, David Hudson II. "A Reading of Evelyn Waugh's *Brideshead Revisited:* A Critical Survey and Thematic Analysis." University of Tulsa, 1968.

841   Wooton, Carl W. "Responses to the Modern World: A Study of Evelyn Waugh's Novels." University of Oregon, 1968. Summary: *Dissertation Abstracts*, 28 (1968), 3693A.

D. Material on General Topics

842   Acton, Harold. *Memoirs of an Aesthete.* London: Methuen and Co., Ltd., 1948.

843   --- *More Memoirs of an Aesthete.* London: Methuen and Co, Ltd., 1970. Pp. 224-226, 304-319, and *passim.* In U.S.,

Memories of an Aesthete 1934-1968. New York: Viking, 1970.

844 Albérès, R. M. "Evelyn Waugh ou de l'humour à l'essentialisme," *Revue de Paris*, 63 (April 1956), No. 4, 83-91.

845 Alexander, Calvert. *The Catholic Literary Revival, Three Phases of its Development from 1845 to the Present.* Milwaukee: Bruce, 1935. Pp. 277-295.

846 Allen, W. Gore. "Evelyn Waugh and Graham Greene," *Irish Monthly*, 77 (January 1949), 16-22.

847 Allen, Walter. *Tradition and Dream: The English and American Novel from the Twenties to Our Time.* London: Phoenix House, 1964. Pp. 208-214. Also published as *The Modern Novel in Britain and the United States.* New York: Dutton, 1964. Pp. 208-214.

847a Allsop, Kenneth, John Davenport and Marie-Louise de Zuleuta. Letters to the editor, *Spectator*, 216 (13 May 1966), 595-598.

847b "Another Author Turns to Rome, Mr. Evelyn Waugh Leaves Church of England, Young Satirist of Mayfair," *Daily Express*, 30 September 1930, p. 1.

847c "Antic antiques. Aldous Huxley; Evelyn Waugh." *Time* (Atlantic ed.) 71, No. 16, (1958), 66, 68.

847d "Authors Take Sides." *Left Review*. London: Writers International, British Section, November 1937.

848 Mr. Gossip [Patrick Balfour]. "And Humiliation" [on Waugh's *Decline and Fall*], *Daily Sketch*, 30 January 1929, p. 5.

849 Mr. Gossip [Patrick Balfour]. On Bruno Hat Affair, *Daily Sketch*, 25 July 1929, p. 5.

850   Mr. Gossip [Patrick Balfour]. "Echoes of the Town" (on Waugh and his trip to Abyssinia), *Daily Sketch,* 10 October 1930, p. 5.

851   Mr. Gossip [Patrick Balfour]. "An Idea; Bottle-Green Bowlers," *Daily Sketch,* 14 January 1930, p. 5.

852   Balfour, Patrick [Lord Kinross]. "Kinross on Waugh on Waugh," *Envoy,* November 1967, pp. 7, 10, 65.

853   Mr. Gossip [Patrick Balfour]. "Preservation of Oxford-- Evelyn Waugh Suggests Dynamite," *Daily Sketch,* 23 February 1930, p. 5.

854   Balfour, Patrick. *Society Racket, A Critical Survey of Modern Social Life.* London: John Long, 1932.

855   Mr. Gossip [Patrick Balfour]. "The Waugh Brothers," [on *Decline and Fall*], *Daily Sketch,* 28 July 1928, p. 5.

856   Lord Kinross [Patrick Balfour]. "The Years with Kinross," (series of 5 weekly chapters in July-August, 1961), *Punch.* References to Waugh on p. 211.

857   Bannington, T. J. "Mr. Waugh's Pieties," *The Bell,* 13 (February 1947), 58-63. Reply to O'Donnell, "The Pieties of Evelyn Waugh."

858   Barnett, William F. "A Thought for the Interim: Evelyn Waugh's remarks on Vatican II," *America,* 108 (30 March 1963), 440-442. See the reply by Martin C. D'Arcy, S. J., *America,* 108 (20 April 1963), 516.

859   Beary, T. J. "Religion and the Modern Novel," *Catholic World,* 166 (December 1947), 203-211.

860   Beaton, Cecil. *The Wandering Years: Diaries: 1922-1939.* London: Weidenfeld and Nicolson, 1961. Pp. 173-174.

861   Beattie, A. M. "Evelyn Waugh," *Canadian Forum,* 33 (1953/54), 226-229.

864   "The Beauty of His Malice: Evelyn Waugh (1903-1966),"
      Time (22 April 1966), 61.

865   Beer, Otto F. "Englische Gegenwartsliteratur: Evelyn
      Waugh," *Universitas*, 7 (1952), 31-34.

866   Benedict, Stewart H. "The Candide Figure in the Novels
      of Evelyn Waugh," *Papers of the Michigan Academy of
      Science, Arts, and Letters*, 48 (1963), 685-690.

866a Benstock, Bernard. "The Present Recaptured: D. H.
      Lawrence and Others," *Southern Review*, 4 (July 1968),
      802-816.

866b Bentley, Nicolas. *A Version of the Truth*. London: Andre
      Deutsch, 1960. P. 99.

867   Bergonzi, Bernard. "Evelyn Waugh's Gentleman," *Crit-
      ical Quarterly*, 5 (1963), 23-36.

868   --- "Evelyn Waugh's *Sword of Honour*," *Listener*, 71 (20
      February 1964), 306-307.

869   --- *The Situation of the Novel* (London: Macmillan, 1970),
      pp. 104-118 and *passim*.

870   Betjeman, John. "The Angry Novelist," *Strand*, 112
      (March 1947), 42, 44. Osbert Lancaster caricature,
      p. 43.

871   --- "Evelyn Waugh: A Critical Study" in *Living Writers,
      Being Critical Studies Broadcast in the B.B.C. Third
      Programme*, ed. Gilbert Phelps. London: Sylvan Press,
      1947. Pp. 137-140.

872   Birkenhead, Lord [Frederick Winston Furneaux Smith].
      Lady Eleanor Smith, A Memoir. London: Hutchinson,
      1953.

873   --- "My Contemporaries," *Harper's Bazaar* (London), 9
      (November 1933), pp. 74, 79. He knew Waugh at Oxford
      and after.

874 Blumenberg, Hans. "Eschatologische Ironie: Uber die Romane Evelyn Waughs," *Hochland*, 46 (1953/54), 241-251; also in Karlheinz Schmidthus (ed.), *Lob der Schopfung und Argernis der Zeit: Moderne christliche Dichtung in Kritik und Deutung* (Freiburg, 1959), pp. 159-170.

875 Bodelsen, C. A. "Evelyn Waugh," in Sven M. Kristensen (ed.), *Fremmede digtere i det 20. arhundrede*, Vol. III (Copenhagen, 1968), pp. 185-198.

876 Borrello, Alfred. "A Visit to Combe Florey: Evelyn Waugh's Home," *Evelyn Waugh Newsletter*, 2, No. 3 (Winter 1968), 1-3.

877 --- "Evelyn Waugh and Erle Stanley Gardner," *Evelyn Waugh Newsletter*, 4, No. 3 (Winter 1970), 1-3.

878 Bowra, C. M. *Memories 1898-1939.* London: Weidenfeld and Nicholson, 1966; Cambridge, Mass.: Harvard University Press, 1967. Pp. 165, 172-176, 250.

879 Boyle, Alexander. "Evelyn Waugh," *Irish Monthly*, 78 (February 1950), 75-81.

880 Boyle, R. "Evelyn Waugh: Master of Satire," *Grail*, 35 (November 1953), 28-32.

881 Brady, Charles A. "Evelyn Waugh: Shrove Tuesday Motley and Lenten Sackcloth," *Catholic Library World*, 16 (March 1945), 163-177, 189.

882 --- "In Memoriam Arthur Evelyn St. John Waugh 1903, 1966," *America*, 194 (1966), 594-595.

883 Brander, Donald M. "Die Romane von Evelyn Waugh: Charaktere als algebraische Figuren in einer irrealen Welt," *Deutsche Universitätszeitung*, 11 (1956), No. 4, 13-15.

884 Braybrooke, Neville. "Evelyn Waugh," *Fortnightly*, NS 171

(March 1952), 197-202; also in *Books on Trial*, 10
(April 1952), 270-271, 299.

885 --- "Evelyn Waugh and Blimp," *Blackfriars*, 33 (1952),
508-512.

886 Breit, Harvey. "An Interview with Evelyn Waugh," *New
York Times Book Review*, 13 March 1949, p. 23; also
in Breit, *The Writer Observed*. London: Redman, 1957.
Pp. 43-46; Cleveland: World, 1957; New York: Collier
Books, 1961. Pp. 34-36.

887 --- "W. Somerset Maugham and Evelyn Waugh," *The Writer
Observed*. Cleveland: World, 1957; London: Redman,
1957. Pp. 147-149; New York: Collier Books, 1961.
Pp. 101-102.

888 " 'Brideshead' Proofs Presented to College," *Greyhound*
(Loyola College, Baltimore) 19 December 1947, p. 1.

889 Brien, Alan. "Permission to Speak, Captain?" *Spectator*,
216 (15 April 1966), 462-463.

890 Brophy, Brigid. *Don't Never Forget*. New York: Holt,
Rinehart & Winston, 1967. Pp. 156-158.

891 "Bruno Hat" affair. *Tatler*, 31 July 1929, p. 192.

892 Buckley, William F. "Evelyn Waugh, R.I.P.," *National
Review*, 18 (3 May 1966), 400, 402.

893 Burgess, Anthony. "The Comedy of Ultimate Truths,"
Spectator, 216 (15 April 1966), 462.

894 --- "La comédie des vérités ultimes," *La Table Ronde*,
No. 220 (May 1966), 8-12.

895 --- *The Novel Now: A Guide to Contemporary Fiction*.
New York: Norton, 1967; London: Faber and Faber,
1967. Pp. 54-58 and *passim*.

896 --- "Waugh Begins" and "The Comedy of Ultimate Truths," *Urgent Copy: Literary Studies*. London: Cape, 1968; New York: Norton, 1969. Pp. 21-29.

897 Butcher, Maryvonne. "Evelyn Waugh: Er machte Kunst und Schlagzeilen," *Dokumente* (Cologne), 22 (1966), 236-238.

898 Calder, Angus. *The People's War: Britain 1939-1945*. New York: Pantheon Books, 1969. References to Waugh pp. 51, 170, 393, 513-514, 560.

899 Cameron, J. M. "A Post-Waugh Insight," *Commonweal*, 83 (29 October 1965), 114-115.

900 --- "Evelyn Waugh, R.I.P," *Commonweal*, 84 (29 April 1966), 167-168.

901 --- "The Catholic Novelist and European Culture," *Twentieth Century Studies*, No. 1 (March 1969), 79-94.

902 Caraman, Philip. "Evelyn Waugh: Panegyric," *Tablet*, 220 (30 April 1966), 518.

903 Carens, James F. "The Year's Work in Waugh Studies," *Evelyn Waugh Newsletter*, 4, i (Spring 1970), 3-6.

904 Carew, Dudley. *The House is Gone, A Personal Retrospect*. London: Robert Hale, 1949. Pp. 80-105, 199.

905 Carstensen, Broder. "Evelyn Waugh and Ernest Hemingway," *Archiv für das Studium der neueren Sprachen und Literaturen*, 190 (1954), 193-203.

906 Casey, George. "Same Always, Please; Evelyn Waugh's Hopes for the Council," *Commonweal*, 77 (1 February 1963), 487-489.

907 Cassen, Bernard. "Evelyn Waugh: la nostalgie d'un ordre qui n'a jamais été," *Le Monde* (Paris), 27 April 1968, pp. iv-v.

908 Cecchin, Giovanni. "Echi di T. S. Eliot nei Romanzi di Evelyn Waugh," *English Miscellany* (Rome), 14 (1963), 237-275.

909 Chamberlain, C. L. "De mortuis nil nisi bonum," *Lancing College Magazine*, Christmas Term, 1942, pp. 126-127.

910 --- "In Memoriam," *Lancing College Magazine*, Summer 1966, pp. 58-60.

911 *Chips: The Diaries of Sir Henry Channon*, ed. Robert Rhodes James. London: Weidenfeld and Nicholson, 1967. Pp. 19, 403.

912 Chastaing, Maxime. "Les romans humoristiques d'Evelyn Waugh," *Esprit* (Paris), 22 (1954), 247-266.

913 --- "Ein Satiriker in Stichworten: Evelyn Waughs gesellschaftskritische Romane," *Wort und Warheit*, 10 (May 1955), 340-355.

914 Christiansen, Arthur. *Headlines All My Life*. New York: Harper, 1961. Reference to Waugh on p. 155.

915 Churchill Randolph. "Evelyn Waugh: Letters (and Post-cards) to Randolph Churchill," *Encounter*, 31 (July 1968), 3-19.

916 Clinton, Farley. "Days of His Pilgrimage: The Religion of Evelyn Waugh," *Triumph*, 2 (4 April 1967), 31-34.

917 --- "Evelyn Waugh, R.I.P." *National Review*, 18 (3 May 1966), 416-417.

918 Cogley, John. "A Suggestion for Mr. Waugh," *Commonweal*, 81 (23 October 1964), 120-122. Replies by Waugh and others, 4 December 1964, pp. 352-354; 18 December 1964, p. 424.

919 Cohen, Nathan, narrator. "A Profile of Evelyn Waugh," C.B.C. radio, 28 October 1969. Unpublished.

920 Collingridge, A. C. Editorial on Oxford University Railway Club, *Isis*, 30 May 1923, p. 1.

921 "Commentary," *Times Literary Supplement*, 1 February 1968, p. 113. Account of *The Scarlet Woman*.

922 Connolly, Cyril. "Apotheosis in Austin," *Sunday Times*, 6 June 1971. Visit to University of Texas; quotes two Waugh items.

923 --- "Three Shelves," *New Statesman and Nation*, 4 January 1936, pp. 25-26.

924 --- "Where Engels Fears to Tread," in *The Condemned Playground, Essays: 1927-1944*. London: Routledge, 1945.

925 --- *Enemies of Promise*. (2nd edition) London: Penquin Books, 1961 [1938]. New York: Macmillan, 1948.

925a --- *Ideas and Places*. London: Weidenfeld and Nicholson, 1953. Pp. 224-225.

926 Conway, Pierre. "Almost," *Commonweal*, 48 (1948), 402-404.

927 Cooper, Diana. *The Light of Common Day*. Boston: Houghton, Mifflin, 1959.

928 --- *Trumpets from the Steep*. London: Rupert Hart-Davis, 1960; Boston: Houghton, Mifflin, 1960. Pp. 29, 212, 214, 221.

929 Corr, Patricia. "Evelyn Waugh: Sanity and Catholicism," *Studies*, 51 (Autumn 1962), 388-399.

930 --- "Evelyn Waugh: Sanity and Catholicism," *Catholic Mind*, 61 (March 1963), 17-22.

931 Cosman, Max. "The Nature and Work of Evelyn Waugh," *Colorado Quarterly*, 4 (Spring 1956), 428-441.

932   Craft, Robert. "Stravinsky and Some Writers," *Harper's*,
      237 (December 1968), 101-108.

933   Cronin, Anthony. "A Tribute to Evelyn Waugh," *Envoy*,
      5 (July 1951), 30-36.

934   "Crowd Hears Waugh Speak," *Greyhound*, 11 February
      1949, p. 1. Title, "A Spiritual Odyssey," on Knox,
      Chesterton, Greene. Photograph of Waugh.

935   D'Arcy, Fr. M. C., and 11 Remonstrants. "Letter to
      Editor: Mr. Evelyn Waugh," *Tablet*, 21 January
      1933, p. 85.

936   Davis, Robert Murray. "Evelyn Waugh's Early Work:
      The Formation of a Method," *Texas Studies in Liter-
      ature and Language*, 7 (1965/66), 97-108.

937   --- "Evelyn Waugh on the Art of Fiction," *Papers on
      Language and Literature*, 2 (1966), 243-252.

938   --- "The Mind and Art of Evelyn Waugh," *Papers on
      Language and Literature*, 3 (1967), 270-287.

939   --- "The Year's Work in Waugh Studies," *Evelyn Waugh
      Newsletter*, 2, i (Spring 1968), 3-5.

940   --- "Textual Problems in the Novels of Evelyn Waugh,"
      Papers of the Bibliographical Society of America, 62
      (1968), 259-263; reprinted, 63 (1969), 41-46.

941   --- "The Shrinking Garden and New Exits: The Comic-
      Satiric Novel in the Twentieth Century," *Kansas
      Quarterly*, 1 (Summer 1969), 5-16.

942   --- "Evelyn Waugh and Brian Howard," *Evelyn Waugh
      Newsletter*, 4 (Autumn 1970), 5-6.

943   Dennis, Nigel. "Evelyn Waugh: The Pillar of Anchorage
      House," *Partisan Review*, 10 (July-August 1943), 350-
      361.

944 Deschner, Karlheinz. "Evelyn Waugh," in Hermann Fried-
mann and Otto Mann (eds.), *Christliche Dichter der
Gegenwart: Beiträge zur europaischen Literatur.*
Heidleberg: Rothe, 1955. Pp. 224-237. Revised edition,
Bern and Munich: Francke, 1968. Pp. 240-252.

945 Dever, Joe. "Echoes of Two Waughs," *Commonweal,* 53
(27 October 1950), 68-70.

946 "Dilettanti, The." *Lancing College Magazine,* December
1919, pp. 107-108.

947 "Dilettanti Society." [Waugh one of original founders
forced to resign upon advancement and is sadly missed],
Lancing College Magazine, March 1921, p. 21.

948 Dollen, Charles. *Vatican II: A Bibliography.* Metuchen,
N. J.: Scarecrow Press, 1969.

949 Domino [?]. "What London Tells Me," "There's a Divinity
Who Shapes our mustaches--But She Likes Them Manly,"
Evening Standard, 4 February 1929, p. 4.

950 Dooley, D. J. "The Council's First Victim," *Triumph,* 5
(June 1970), 33-35.

951 --- "Strategy of the Catholic Novelist," *Catholic World,*
189 (July 1959), 300-304.

952 --- "Waugh and Black Humor," *Evelyn Waugh Newsletter,*
2 (Autumn 1968), 1-3.

953 Doyle, Paul A. "The Persecution of Evelyn Waugh,"
America, 99 (3 May 1958), 165, 168-169.

954 --- "The Church, History, and Evelyn Waugh," *The American Benedictine Review,* 9 (Autumn-Winter 1958/59),
202-208.

955 --- "The Politics of Waugh," *Renascence,* 11 (Summer
1959), 171-174, 221.

956 --- "Evelyn Waugh," *Critical Quarterly*, 2 (Autumn 1960), 269-270. Reply to Dyson, "Evelyn Waugh and the Mysteriously Disappearing Hero."

957 --- "Brideshead Rewritten," *Catholic Book Reporter*, 2 (May 1962), 9-10.

958 --- "The Year's Work in Waugh Studies," *Evelyn Waugh Newsletter*, 3, i (Spring 1969), 6-8.

959 --- "Evelyn Waugh's Attitude Toward Ecumenism," *Twin Circle*, 3 (27 July 1969), 1, 11-12.

960 Driberg, Tom. *The Best of Both Worlds: A Personal Diary.* London: Phoenix House, 1953. P. 52.

961 --- [Dragoman]. "Less Serious" [in "The Talk of London" col.], *Daily Express*, 18 September 1928, p. 19.

962 --- [Dragoman]. On Bruno Hat affair, *Daily Express*, 24 July 1929, p. 15.

963 --- [Dragoman]. "The Talk of London" (on Waugh and Lady Lavery, just prior to his going to Abyssinia), *Daily Express*, 8 October 1930, p. 19.

964 --- [Dragoman]. An item on Waugh's "Futurist" Christmas card, *Daily Express*, 24 December 1930, p. 9.

965 --- [William Hickey]. An item quoting Waugh's remark that travel books are out because of Fleming's, *Daily Express*, 3 September 1934, p. 6.

966 Dyson, A. E. "Evelyn Waugh and the Mysteriously Disappearing Hero," *Critical Quarterly*, 2 (Spring 1960), 72-79. See reply by Doyle, "Evelyn Waugh."

967 --- "Evelyn Waugh and the Mysteriously Disappearing Hero," *The Crazy Fabric: Essays in Irony.* London: Macmillan, 1965; New York: St. Martin's Press, 1965. Pp. 187-196. Revised version of *Critical Quarterly* article.

968 Eagleton, Terry. "Evelyn Waugh and the Upper-Class Novel," in *Exiles and Emigres: Studies in Modern Literature*. New York: Schocken Books, 1970. Pp. 33-70. [42-70 on Waugh himself].

969 Edwards, John D. "Fleurs blanches et ours en peluche," *Le Monde* (Paris), 27 April 1968, p. iv.

970 Eimerl, Sarel. "The Why of Waugh," *Reporter*, 38 (2 May 1968), 38, 40.

971 Ellis, G. U. *Twilight on Parnassus: A Survey of Post-War Fiction and Pre-War Criticism*. London: Michael Joseph, Ltd., 1939. Pp. 370-385.

972 "Engagement," *Lancing College Magazine*, March 1937, p. 16. [Waugh engaged to marry Laura Herbert.]

973 "Evelyn Waugh," *Wilson Library Bulletin*, 5 (April 1931), 488.

974 [Evelyn Waugh attacks dialogue with separated brethren in letter to London *Tablet*], *Clayman*, 77 (November 1963), 27.

975 "Evelyn Waugh R.I.P.," *America*, 114 (23 April 1966), 578.

976 "Evelyn Waugh to Give Talk," *Greyhound* (Loyola College, Baltimore), 14 January 1949, p. 1. The date of the talk was February 8.

977 Farr, D. Paul. "The Edwardian Golden Age and Nostalgic Truth," *Dalhousie Review*, 50 (Autumn 1970), 378-393.

978 --- "Evelyn Waugh: Tradition and a Modern Talent," *South Atlantic Quarterly*, 68 (1969), 506-519.

979 "Father Talbot Inaugurated as President," *Greyhound* (Loyola College, Baltimore), 5 December 1947, pp. 1, 2.

980   Faulkner, William. *Essays, Speeches and Public Letters, etc*, ed. James R. Meriweather. New York: Random House, 1965. Pp. 210-211. Same as item 981.

981   --- Letter to the Editor, *Time*, 56 (13 November 1950), 6. Supports EW on *Across the River and into the Trees*.

982   Featherstone, Joseph. "The Ordeal of Evelyn Waugh," *New Republic*, 155, ii-iii (16 July 1966), 21-23.

983   Ferri, Paola. "Evelyn Waugh e la narrativa cattolica inglese," *Vita e Pensiero*, 42 (1959), 831-838.

984   Fielding, Daphne. *Mercury Presides*. London: Eyre and Spottiswoode, 1954; New York: Harcourt, Brace, 1955. Pp. 105, 202, 214.

985   --- *Those Remarkable Cunards: Emerald and Nancy*. New York: Athenaeum, 1968. P. 136.

986   Fielding, Gabriel. "Evelyn Waugh: the price of satire," *Listener*, 72 (8 October 1964), 541-542.

987   --- "Evelyn Waugh and the Cross of Satire," *The Critic*, 23 (February-March 1965), 52-56.

988   Fleming, Robert Peter [Strix]. "Patronage at Piers Court," *Spectator*, 193 (6 August 1954), 160.

989   Flood, E. "Jungmann Revisited, or a Word to Mr. Waugh" [review of Jungmann's *Pastoral Liturgy* and of Waugh's *Spectator* article], *Life Spirit*, 17 (March 1963), 383-387.

990   Fraser, G. S. *The Modern Writer and His World*. London: D. Verschoyle, 1953. Pp. 109-113. Revised edition London, 1964. Pp. 141-144; New York: F. A. Praeger, 1965.

991   Fremantle, Anne. *Three-Cornered Heart*. New York: Viking, 1970. Pp. 286-292.

992 --- "Waugh in America," *Vogue*, 136 (15 November 1960), 54, 65-66.

993 Fricker, Robert. *Der Moderne englische Roman*. Gottingen: Vandenhoeck and Ruprecht, revised edition, 1966. Pp. 196-203.

994 Fytton, Francis. "Waugh-Fare," *Catholic World*, 181 (1955), 349-355.

995 Gadd, Thomas W. Letter to the Editor, *Spectator*, 216 (22 April 1966), 495. Cites letters from Waugh.

996 Gardiner, Harold C. "Waugh's Awry Critics," *America*, 74 (12 January 1946), 409-410.

997 --- "Follow-up on Waugh," *America*, 74 (16 February 1946), 536.

998 Gate-Crasher as Zulu, The." [Photograph of Waugh and wife at "Tropical Party"], *Bystander*, 17 July 1929, pp. 178-179.

999 "Gazette, La." [Quips about *"Noah, or the Future of Drunkenness"* and *"Abraham, or the Future of Strange Vices"*], *Cherwell*, 7 May 1927, p. 4.

1000 "Gazette, La." In the column "The Wanderer Returns," *Cherwell*, 24 October 1925, p. 24.

1001 "General." *Lancing College Magazine*, July 1936, p. 77.

1001a Gerhardie, William. "The Ordeal of Evelyn Waugh," *Times Literary Supplement*, 12 October 1967, p. 961. [Gerhardie is return to ancestral spelling of the novelist's name].

1002 Glanz, Luzia. "Der Mensch und die Eschata: Gedanken zu Dichtungen von Evelyn Waugh, Clive Staples Lewis, Edzard Schaper und Boris Pasternak," in Hermann Kirchoff (ed.), *Kaufet die Zeit aus: Beitrage zur christlichen Eschatologie: Festgabe fur Theoderich Kampmann.* Paderborn: Schöningh, 1959. Pp. 113-132.

1003 Gleason, James. "Evelyn Waugh and the Stylistics of Commitment," *Wisconsin Studies in Literature,* No. 2 (1965), 70-74.

1004 Glen, Alexander R. *Young Men in the Arctic, The Oxford University Arctic Expedition.* London: Faber and Faber, 1935. Pp. 227-260.

1005 Goldring, Douglas. *The Nineteen Twenties: A General Survey and some Personal Memories.* London: Nicholson and Watson, 1945. On Waugh, pp. 99, 112, 212, 225.

1006 --- *Odd Man Out: The Autobiography of a Propaganda Novelist.* London: Chapman and Hall, 1935. Pp. 282-283.

1007 Götz, Karl-August. "Die Romane von Evelyn Waugh," *Die Anregung* (Cologne), 8 (1956), Beilage pp. 40-43.

1008 Gordon, Caroline. "Some Readings and Misreadings," *Sewanee Review,* 61 (1953), 384-407.

1009 Grace, William J. "Evelyn Waugh as a Social Critic," *Renascence,* 1, ii (Spring 1949), 28-40.

1010 Green, Martin. "British Comedy and The British Sense of Humour: Shaw, Waugh, and Amis," *Texas Quarterly,* 4 (Autumn 1961), 217-227.

1011 Greene, George. "Scapegoat With Style: The Status of Evelyn Waugh," *Queen's Quarterly,* 71 (Autumn 1964), 485-493.

1012 Greene, Graham. "Plenty of Good Novels," *Everyman,* 30 October 1930, pp. 419-420.

1013 --- Note to Waugh obituary, *Times*, 15 April 1966, p. 15. Reprinted as "Graham Greene's Tribute," *Evelyn Waugh Newsletter*, 1, i (Spring 1967), 1.

1014 Greenidge, Terence L. "The Cinematograph in Oxford-- A Record of a Year's Work and an Appeal," *Isis*, 17 June 1925, pp. 10-12.

1015 --- "Concerning Certain Pilgrims' Progress," *Isis*, 15 October 1924, p. 8.

1016 --- *Degenerate Oxford? A Critical Study of Modern University Life.* London: Chapman and Hall, 1930.

1017 --- "The Story of Oxford Films," *Isis*, 24 November 1926, pp. 10-11.

1018 Gribble, Thomas. "Recent BBC Productions of Waugh Stories," *Evelyn Waugh Newsletter*, 5, i (Spring 1971), 5-6.

1019 Griffiths, Joan. "Waugh's Problem Comedies," *Accent*, 9 (Spring 1949), 165-170.

1020 Grimley, Fr. Bernard. "News and Views" (on Waugh's conversion), *Catholic Gazette*, December 1930, p. 371.

1021 "Grosvenor, John." "Now Which is It?" (on Agatha Runcible's being composite of Elizabeth Ponsonby and Babe Plunkett-Greene), *Sunday Dispatch*, 16 March 1930, p. 4.

1022 "Group at Opening of Campion Hall, Oxford," *Catholic Herald*, 3 July 1936, p. 3. Photograph of Waugh, Mrs. Mary Herbert, et al.

1022a Guenther, John. "The Ordeal of Evelyn Waugh," *Times Literary Supplement*, 14 September 1967, p. 819.

1023 Gutteridge, Bernard. "Wine with Mr. Waugh," *New Statesman and Nation*, 44 (30 August 1952), 233.

1024 C. B. H. "Is Life Worth Living?" (on Waugh's serious laughter), *Cherwell*, 31 May 1930, p. 111.

1025 Hall, James. "The Other Post-War Rebellion: Evelyn Waugh Twenty-Five Years After," *ELH*, 28 (1961), 187-202.

1026 --- Stylized Rebellion: Evelyn Waugh," *The Tragic Comedians: Seven Modern British Novelists*. Bloomington: Indiana University Press, 1963. Pp. 45-65. Revised version of *ELH* article.

1027 Hamnett, Nina. *Is She a Lady? A Problem in Autobiography*. London: Alan Wingate, 1955.

1028 Handford, Basil W. T. *Lancing: A History of SS. Mary and Nicholas College, Lancing, 1848-1930*. Oxford: Basil Blackwell, 1933. Pp. 274, 278, 279.

1029 Hansen-Löve, Friedrich. "Quomodo sedet sola civitas," *Wort und Wahrheit*, 3 (1948), 716-720.

1030 Harrington, Edmund. Photograph of Hon. Mrs. Evelyn Waugh in Cairo, *Bystander*, 24 April 1929, p. 169.

1031 Harris, M. G. Letter to the Editor (on E. W.'s fondness for letters which provoked replies), *Lancing College Magazine*, Christmas Term, 1942, p. 171.

1032 Hart, Jeffrey. "The Seriousness of Evelyn Waugh," *National Review*, 16 (29 December 1964), 1152-1153.

1033 --- "A Touch of Chrism," *Triumph*, ·5 (June 1970), 28-30, 32-33.

1034 "Hawthornden Prize, The." *Tablet*, 27 June 1936, p. 828 .

1035 Haynes, E. S. P. *The Lawyer: A Conversation Piece*. London: Eyre and Spottiswoode, 1951. Pp. 291-293.

1036 Hennessy, C. P. "Evelyn Waugh," *Phoenix*, Autumn 1946, pp. 29-32.

1037 Hillier, Bevis. "When Evelyn Waugh joked with his Publisher," *Times*, 15 July 1968, p. 8.

1038 Hinchcliffe, Peter. "Fathers and Children in the Novels of Evelyn Waugh," *University of Toronto Quarterly*, 35 (1966), 293-310.

1039 Hines, Leo. "Waugh and His Critics," *Commonweal*, 76 (13 April 1962), 60-63.

1040 Hoehn, Matthew (ed.). *Catholic Authors, Contemporary Biographical Sketches*. Newark: St. Mary's Abbey, 1948.

1041 Hohoff, Curt. "Satire als Zeugnis oder Der Romancier Evelyn Waugh," *Wort und Wahrheit*, 7 (1952), 39-44; also in *Geist und Ursprung: Zur moderen Literatur*. Munich: Ehrenwirth, 1954. Pp. 218-227.

1042 Hollis, Christopher. *Along the Road to Frome*. London: George G. Harrap and Co., Lrd., 1958. References to Waugh on pp. 58, 61, 62, 65, and 230.

1043 [Hollis, Christopher]. "Mr. Evelyn Waugh: Artist in Satiric Prose," obituary, *Times*, 11 April 1966, p. 10. Identified by Auberon Waugh in "Death in the Family."

1044 Holman-Hunt, Diana. *My Grandfather, His Wives and Loves*. New York: W. W. Norton, 1969. Pp. 13-17, 20-26 and *passim*.

1045 "Home Hints" [cracks about pate de foie gras and Waugh and about coal scuttles], *Cherwell*, 11 May 1929, p. 43.

1046 Hopeful [probably Waugh]. Letter to the Editor [wants to bury in obscurity the two numbers of L.C.M. of Waugh's editorship, and one of Dudley Carew], *Lancing College Magazine*, March 1922, p. 30.

1047   Horne, Roger. *"Facts, Mr. Waugh,"* *Cherwell*, 13 June
       1936, p. 164.

1048   Hortmann, Wilhelm. *Englische Literatur im 20. Jahrhun-*
       dert. Bern and Munich: Francke, 1965. Pp. 115-
       118, 146-147.

1049   "House Notes" [Head's has lost Waugh; he is congrat-
       ulated on winning Hertford Scholarship on "little
       more than a term's hard work"], *Lancing College*
       Magazine, February 1922, p. 8.

1050   "How Waugh wrecked the Aristocracy with *Handful,"*
       Cherwell, Fall 1936, p. 143.

1051   Howarth, Herbert. "Quelling the Riot: Evelyn Waugh's
       Progress," in Harry J. Mooney and Thomas F. Staley
       (eds.), *The Shapeless God: Essays on Modern Fiction*.
       Pittsburgh: University of Pittsburgh Press, 1968. Pp.
       67-89.

1052   Hrastnik, H. "Porträt Evelyn Waughs," *Die Presse*
       (Vienna), 6 (27 January 1951).

1053   "Hypocrites' Film, The," *Isis*, 14 May 1924, p. 4.

1054   "If Gossip We Must," [a column, on Bruno Hat], *By-*
       stander, 7 August 1929, p. 302.

1055   "Intimacies" [Frank Pakenham?], *Oxford University*
       Review, 2 (9 February 1926), 42.

1056   "Isis Idol" [on his history tutor Cruttwell], *Isis*, 5 March
       1924, pp. 7-8.

1057   Isham, Gyles. Editorial on "Movies," *Isis*, 24 October
       1923, pp. 1-2.

1058   James, S. B. "Evelyn Waugh's Apologia," *Missionary*,
       44 (December 1930), 415-417.

1059 Jarrett, Bede. "Waughs and Rumours of Waughs," *Black-friars*, 2 (March 1922), 716-723.

1060 Johnson, Robert V. "The Early Novels of Evelyn Waugh," in John Colmer (ed.), *Approaches to the Novel*. Edinburgh and London: Oliver and Boyd, 1967. Pp. 78-89.

1061 Karl, Frederick R. "The World of Evelyn Waugh: The Normally Insane," *A Reader's Guide to the Contemporary English Novel*. New York: Noonday Press, 1962. Pp. 167-182; London: Thames and Hudson, 1963. Pp. 167-182.

1062 Kellogg, Gene. "The Catholic Novel in Convergence," *Thought*, 45 (Summer 1970), 265-296.

1063 --- "Evelyn Waugh," *The Vital Tradition: the Catholic Novel in a Period of Convergence*. Chicago: Loyola University Press, 1970. Pp. 101-110, and *passim*.

1064 Kenner, Hugh. "Evelyn Waugh: In Memoriam," *National Review*, 18 (1966), 418.

1065 Kenny, H. A. "Evelyn Waugh and the Novel," *Magnificat*, 92 (1953), 278-280.

1066 Kermode, Frank. "Mr. Waugh's Cities," *Encounter*, 15 (November 1960), 63-70; also in Kermode, *Puzzles and Epiphanies: Essays and Reviews 1958-1961*. New York: Chilmark Press, 1962. Pp. 164-175; London: Routledge and Kegan Paul, 1962.

1067 Kernan, Alvin B. "The Wall and the Jungle: The Early Novels of Evelyn Waugh," *Yale Review*, 53 (1963/64), 199-220.

1068 --- "Running in Circles: The Early Novels of Evelyn Waugh," *The Plot of Satire*. New Haven: Yale University Press, 1965. Pp. 143-167. Revised version of *Yale Review* article.

1069   Kleine, Don W. "The Cosmic Comedies of Evelyn Waugh,"
       South Atlantic Quarterly, 61 (1962), 533-539.

1070   Knox, Oliver. "A Desperate Conversation with Evelyn,"
       Cornhill, Nos. 1057-1058 (Autumn-Winter 1968-1969),
       181-184.

1071   --- "No ... er Creme de Menthe: A Desperate Conversation
       with Evelyn Waugh," Cyril Ray (ed.), *The Compleat
       Imbiber 10.* London: Hutchinson, 1969. Pp. 26-29.

1072   Konody, P. G. "ART and artists" (on exhibit of the
       Lamb portrait of Waugh), *Observer,* 15 November 1931,
       p. 12.

1073   Kranz, Gisbert. "Vier grobe Erzähler aus christlichem
       Geist: Sigrid Undset, Werner Bergengruen, Graham
       Greene, Evelyn Waugh," *Die Kirche in der Welt*
       (Münster), 11 (1960), 357-370.

1074   --- *Europas christliche Literatur.* Paderborn: Schöningh,
       1968. Pp. 492- 495.

1075   [Kunitz, Stanley J.]. Tante, Dilly (ed.), *Living Authors*.
       New York: H. W. Wilson, 1931. Pp. 426-427.

1076   LaFrance, Marston. "The Earliest Waugh Reference
       Known," *Evelyn Waugh Newsletter,* 5 (Autumn 1971),
       8-9.

1077   Lambotte, Charles. "Un humoriste: Evelyn Waugh," in
       F. Lelotte (ed.), *Convertis du XXe siecle,* Vol. 2.
       Paris: Castermann; Brussels: Foyer Notre-Dame, 1952.
       Pp. 71-86.

1077a Lancaster, Marie Jacqueline, ed. *Brian Howard: Portrait
       of a Failure.* London: Blond, 1968. Pp. 195-199, 375 -
       377 and *passim.*

1078   *Lancing Register, The.* Third Edition, Revised and Con-
       tinued to 1932. Cambridge, England: Cambridge Uni-
       versity Press, 1933.

1079   Lane, Calvin W. "Waugh's Book Reviews for *Night and Day*," *Evelyn Waugh Newsletter*, 4, i (Spring 1970), 1-3.

1080   Lapicque, F. "La satire dans l'oeuvre d'Evelyn Waugh," *Études Anglaises*. 10 (July-September 1957), 193-215.

1081   "L.C.D.S.." [Lancing College Debate Society]. [Waugh on the "Debate Committee"], *Lancing College Magazine*, February 1921, pp. 5-6.

1082   Lehmann, John. *A Nest of Tigers: Edith, Osbert and Sacheverell Sitwell in their times.* London: Macmillan, 1968. Pp. 5, 81, 114-115, 252-256, 275; Boston: Little, Brown, 1968.

1082a   Lennartz, Franz. *Ausländische Dichter und Schriftsteller unserer Zeit: Einzeldarstellungen zur Schönen Literatur in fremden Sprachen.* Stuttgart: Kröner, 3rd edition, 1960. Pp. 714-718.

1083   Leo, J. "Evelyn Waugh versus the Ecumenical Council," *Catholic Messenger*, 8 (27 December 1962), 10.

1084   Lewis, Percy Wyndham. *Doom of Youth.* London: Chatto and Windus, 1932. Pp. 99, 106-109, 161.

1085   "Library, the." *Lancing College Magazine*, April 1920, pp. 20-21. [An Illuminated Prayer. Won Mention at Exhibition of Fall Term 1919, Lancing College.]

1086   "Library Notes." *Lancing College Magazine*, June 1919, p. 39. [An Illuminated Missal. Won First Prize at Exhibition of Easter Term 1919, Lancing College.]

1087   "Library Notes." *Lancing College Magazine*, February 1921, pp. 6-7. [On Writing Exhibits, "Study Typical of the Decadent School," and "Landscape in Greens." Shared First Prize at Exhibition of Fall Term 1920, Lancing College.]

1088 Lister, R. F., Secretary. "L.C.D.S." [President Waugh and Committee made "closed" society], *Lancing College Magazine*, November 1921, p. 76.

1089 "L.C.D.S." [President Waugh avoids taking action of L.C.D.S. closure], *Lancing College Magazine*, December 1921, p. 92.

1091 "Library Notes" [Waugh is Librarian for the term], *Lancing College Magazine*, November 1921, p. 77.

1092 "Library Notes" and "O.L. News" [Duckworth's presented the Library a copy of Waugh's *Rossetti*], *Lancing College Magazine*, Spring 1928, pp. 89, 95.

1093 Linck, Charles E. "Waugh Letters at the Texas Academic Center," *Evelyn Waugh Newsletter*, 1 (Winter 1967), 1-5.

1094 --- "The Year's Work in Waugh Studies, Part 1," *Evelyn Waugh Newsletter*, 5, i (Spring 1971), 1-3.

1095 Linklater, Eric. "Evelyn Waugh," *The Art of Adventure*. London: Macmillan, 1948. Pp. 44-58.

1096 --- "An Urn for Evelyn Waugh," *Time and Tide*, 29 (1948), 1222-1223.

1097 Long, Richard A. and Iva G. Jones. "Towards a Definition of the 'Decadent Novel,' " *College English*, 22 (January 1961), 245-249.

1098 Lorda Alaiz, F. M. "De romanschrijver Evelyn Waugh," *Raam*, No. 12 (1964), 13-29.

1098a Lunn, Arnold. "The Genius of Evelyn Waugh," *Duckett's Register*, 17 (January 1962), 1-2.

1099 --- "Evelyn Waugh Revisited," *National Review*, 20 (27 February 1968), 189-190, 205. In expanded form in Lunn's *Unkilled for So Long*. London: Allen and

Unwin, 1968. Pp. 78-82.

1100 M., C. [On Hypocrites' Club and Others.] *Isis*, 14 May 1924, p. 17.

1102 Maguire, C. J. "Catholic Letters Waste a Weapon," *America*, 68 (10 October 1942), 17-18.

1103 Macauley, Rose. "Evelyn Waugh," *Horizon*, 14 (December 1946), 360-376. Also in: Denys Val Baker (ed.), *Writers of To-day 2*. London: Sidgwick and Jackson, Ltd., 1948. Pp. 135-152.

1104 McCormick, John. *Catastrophe and Imagination: An Interpretation of the Recent English and American Novel*. London: Longmans, 1957. Pp. 286-289.

1105 McLaren, Moray. Comment on obituary, *Times*, 12 April 1966, p. 10.

1106 Marcus, Steven. "Evelyn Waugh and the Art of Entertainment," *Partisan Review*, 23 (Summer 1956), 348-357.

1107 Markovíc, Vida E. "Tony Last," *The Changing Face: Disintegration of Personality in the Twentieth-Century British Novel, 1900-1950*. Carbondale, Illinois: Southern Illinois University Press, 1970. Pp. 70-81.

1108 Marshall, Bruce. "Graham Greene and Evelyn Waugh: Grimness and Gaiety and Grace in Our Times," *Commonweal*, 51 (3 March 1950), 551-553.

1109 --- "Graham Greene e Evelyn Waugh," *Vita e Pensiero*, 35 (1952), 471-474.

1110 Martin, Graham. "Novelists of Three Decades: Evelyn Waugh, Graham Greene, C. P. Snow," in Boris Ford (ed.), *The Modern Age*, The Pelican Guide to English Literature, Vol. 7. 2nd edition., Harmondsworth: Penquin Books, 1963. Pp. 394-414.

1111   Mehoke, James S. "Sartre's Theory of Emotion and
        Three English Novelists: Waugh, Greene, and Amis,"
        Wisconsin Studies in Literature, No. 3 (1966), 105-
        113.

1112   Metzger, Joseph. *Das katholische Schrifttum im heutigen
        England.* Munich: Kösel and Putstet, 1937. Pp. 343-
        344.

1113   Meyer, Heinrich, "Evelyn Waugh (1903-66)," *Books
        Abroad*, 40 (1966), 410-411.

1114   Mikes, George. "Evelyn Waugh," *Eight Humorists*. Lon-
        don: Allan Wingate, 1954. Pp. 127-146.

1115   "Mr. Evelyn Waugh and *The Daily Mail*," *Tablet*, 19
        August 1939, p. 250.

1116   Mitford, Jessica. *Daughters and Rebels.* Boston: Hough-
        ton, Mifflin, 1960.

1117   Mitford, Nancy. "Nancy Mitford's Commentary," *Evelyn
        Waugh Newsletter*, 1, i (Spring 1967), 1-2.

1118   "Modern Play Reading Society." [Waugh is first in
        "closed" society that read *Candida, Gay Lord Quex,*
        and *Honeymoon*], *Lancing College Magazine*, Decem-
        ber 1920, p. 101.

1118a   "Modern Play Reading Society." [Waugh in "closed"
        society that read *Milestones* and *Pygmalion*], *Lancing
        College Magazine*, March 1921, p. 21.

1119   "Modern Play Reading Society." [Waugh in "closed"
        society that read *Paola and Francesca, His Excel-
        lency the Governor,* and *The Choice*], *Lancing Col-
        lege Magazine*, July 1921, p. 60.

1120   "Modern Play Reading Society." [Waugh in "closed"
        society that read *Dandy Dick, The Silver Box,* and
        The Devil's Disciple], *Lancing College Magazine*,

December 1921, pp. 92-93.

1121   Monod, Sylvère. "Satire ou invective?," *Le Monde* (Paris), 27 April 1968, pp. iv-v.

1122   Mosley, Nicholas, "A New Puritanism," *The European*, No. 3 (May 1953), 28-40. Reply to Neame, "Black and Blue."

1123   Mowat, Charles Loch. *Britain Between the Wars, 1918-1940.* Chicago: University of Chicago Press, 1955.

1124   Muggeridge, Malcolm. "Evelyn Waugh," *Observer* [London], 17 April 1966, p. 26.

1125   --- "Evelyn Waugh, Esq.," *The Critic*, 24 (June-July 1966), 56-58.

1126   --- "My Fair Gentleman," *Tread Softly, For You Tread on My Jokes.* London and Glasgow: Fontana, 1969. P. 124.

1127   --- "Zum Tode des englischen Schriftstellers Evelyn Waugh," *Die Zeit*, 21 No. 17 (1966), 19.

1128   Neame, A. J. "Black and Blue: A Study of the Catholic Novel," *The European* No. 3 (April 1953), 26-36. See reply by Mosley, "A New Puritanism."

1129   Neill, D. G., and F. C. Johnston. "The Catholic Novelists," *National Review*, 132 (1949), 345. Reply to Bayley, "Two Catholic Novelists."

1129a Nemoianu, Virgil. "Negatie si afirmat io La Evelyn Waugh [Negation and Assertion with Evelyn Waugh]" in Roumanian translation of *Decline and Fall, Declin și prabușire*, 1968. Pp. 7-20.

1130   Nettesheim, Josefine. "Gnade und Freiheit: 1st Evelyn Waughs Weg zur Kirche eine Sensation?" *Die Friedens-*

stadt (Paderborn) 14 (1951), 47-50.

1131 Newnham, Anthony. "Evelyn Waugh's Library," *Library Chronicle of the University of Texas*, NS, No. 1 (March 1970), 25-29.

1132 Nichols, Beverley. *All I Could Never Be, Some Recollections.* New York: E. P. Dutton, 1952.

1133 --- "Interlude with Evelyn Waugh," *The Sun in My Eyes.* London: Heinemann, 1969. Pp. 265-274.

1134 --- *The Sweet and Twenties.* London: Weidenfeld and Nicolson, 1958.

1135 Nichols, James W. "Romantic and Realistic: The Tone of Evelyn Waugh's Early Novels," *College English*, 24 (October 1962), 46, 51-56.

1136 Nicolson, Harold. *Diaries and Letters: 1930-1939*, ed. Nigel Nicolson. New York: Athenaeum, 1966. P. 53.

1137 Nott, Kathleen. "Evelyn Waugh and the Religious Novel," pp. 26-33 in *The Rationalist Annual* (1959), ed. Hector Hawton. London: Watts and Co., 1959.

1138 Oakes, Philip [Atticus]. Comments on the "Waugh Industry," *Sunday Times*, 8 October 1967, p. 13.

1139 O'Donnell, Donat [Conor Cruise O'Brien]. "The Pieties of Evelyn Waugh," *The Bell*, 13 (December 1946), 38-49; also in *Kenyon Review*, 9 (1947), 400-411; also in John Crowe Ransom (ed.), *The Kenyon Critics*. Cleveland: World, 1951. Pp. 88-98. See reply by Bannington, "Mr. Waugh's Pieties"; and O'Donnell's answer, *The Bell*, 13 (March 1947), 57-62.

1140 --- "The Pieties of Evelyn Waugh," *Maria Cross: Imaginative Patterns in a Group of Modern Catholic Writers.* New York: Oxford University Press, 1952. Pp. 119-134. New edition, under O'Brien's real name, London :

Burns and Oates, 1963. Pp. 109-123. Revised version of *The Bell* article.

1141 O'Faolain, Sean. "Huxley and Waugh: or I do not think, therefore I am," *The Vanishing Hero: Studies in Novelists of the Twenties.* Boston: Atlantic, Little, Brown, 1956. Pp. 31-69; London: Eyre and Spottiswoode, 1957.

1143 Oldmeadow, Earnest. "News and Notes," *Tablet,* 19 October 1935, p. 490. On Waugh's doubtful reporting.

1144 "On with the Dance," [about Waugh and *Friendship*], *Bystander,* 3 July 1929, pp. 4-5.

1145 Onions, A. R. [Berta Ruck]. *A Story-Teller tells the Truth, Reminiscences and Notes.* London: Hutchinson, 1935.

1146 Oppel, Horst. "Englische Erzählkunst: III. Zwischen Chaos und Erlösung," *Die Lebenden Fremdsprachen,* III (1951), 100-112.

1147 Orwell, George. *Collected Essays, Journalism and Letters of George Orwell.* Sonia Orwell and Ian Argus, eds. 4 volumes. London: Secker and Warburg, 1968; New York: Harcourt, Brace and World, 1968. Volume I, pp. 515, 523; Volume III, pp. 63, 248, 283, 339, 372; Volume IV, pp. 438, 442, 478-479, 481, 482, 512-513, 520.

1148 Osborne, John. "Evelyn Waugh Faces *Life* and Vice Versa," *Atlantic,* 218 (December 1966), 114-115.

1149 "O. T. C. Notes" [Waugh appt. Lance Corporal]. *Lancing College Magazine,* November 1921, p. 74.

1150 "Oxford Arts Club" [Waugh on Hanging Committee], *Isis,* 7 May 1924, p. 4.

1151 "Oxford Letter" [E. A. St. J. Waugh at Hertford with

O. L.'s J. N. C. Ford, F. E. Ford, A. R. Martley,
F. M. Hamerton, E. M. B. Southwell--he is only
O. L. representative at Oxford Union Society],
Lancing College Magazine, March 1922, pp. 25-27.

1152 "Oxford Letter" [Waugh is Union Speaker, business
manager of *Oxford Fortnightly Review*, and is witty
at the expense of P. F. Machin], *Lancing College
Magazine*, December 1922, pp. 119-120.

1153 "Oxford Letter" [Waugh the ornament, pillar and blue
suit owner], *Lancing College Magazine*, December
1923, pp. 125-126.

1154 Pakenham, Lord [Earl of Longford]. *Born to Believe.*
London: J. Cape, 1953.

1155 Pakenham, Frank, Earl of Longford. *Five Lives.* London: Hutchinson, 1964. Pp. 14-15, 16, 105, 196.

1156 Pares, Richard [M. Le Feu Chef du Gare]. "The Oxford
University Railway Club," *Cherwell*, 8 December
1923, p. 142.

1157 Parker, Kenneth. " 'Quantitative Judgements Don't
Apply,' " *English Studies in Africa*, 9 (1966), 192-
201.

1158 Patmore, Derek. *Private History: An Autobiography.*
London: Johnathan Cape, 1960. Pp. 145, 169.

1159 Patterson, I. M. "Critic to Critic," *America*, 74 (2 February 1946), 503. Reply to Gardiner, "Waugh's Awry
Critics."

1160 Pearson, Kenneth. "Waugh's Scoop for Harry Worth,"
Sunday Times, 4 July 1971, p. 19.

1161 "People," *Time*, 56 (30 October 1950), 44. Quotes from
Waugh's Review of Hemingway's *Across the River
and into the Trees.*

1162   Photograph of E. Waugh and wife at " Tropical Party,"
         Tatler, 24 July 1929, p. 145.

1163   Photograph of Arthur, Alec and Evelyn Waugh. *Vanity
         Fair*, 30 February 1933, p. 30. In photo-essay on
         literary families.

1163a   Powell, Anthony. "A Memoir," *Adam*, Nos. 301-303
         (1966), 7-9.

1165   Prescott, Orville. "Satirists: Waugh, Marquand," *In My
         Opinion: An Inquiry into the Contemporary Novel*.
         Indianapolis: Bobbs-Merrill, 1952. Pp. 165-179.

1166   Pritchett, V. S. "Evelyn Waugh," *New Statesman*, 71
         (15 April 1966), 547.

1167   --- "Mr. Waugh's Exile," *New Statesman*, 68 (25 Septem-
         ber 1964), 445-446.

1168   "Prize List, 1922" [Waugh won "English Verse" and
         "Scarlyn-Wilson English Literature Prize"], *Lancing
         College Magazine*, February 1922, p. 7.

1169   "Profile: Evelyn Waugh," *World and Press* (December
         1964), 3.

1171   Pryce-Jones, Alan. "Evelyn Waugh," *Commonweal*, 81
         (4 December 1964), 343-345.

1172   Quennell, Peter. "Evelyn Waugh," *New York Times
         Book Review*, 8 May 1966, pp. 2, 33. Also in *Page
         2: The Best of "Speaking of Books" from the New
         York Times Book Review*, ed. Francis Brown. New
         York: Holt, Rinehart, and Winston, 1969. Pp. 260-
         264.

1173   --- "New Novels" (review of A. Powell's *Agents and
         Patients*), *New Statesman and Nation*, 11 January
         1936, p. 54. [Waugh the only modern novelist who
         has made satirical romance his own--seeks refuge

under mother church; on 'malaise' ...]

1174 --- *The Sign of the Fish*. London: Collins, 1960; New York: Viking, 1960. Pp. 60, 63-64.

1175 Ray, Cyril. Notes to the obituary, *Times*, 15 April 1966, p. 15.

1176 Raymond, John. "Waugh's Last Post," *New Statesman*, 71 (1966), 608-609.

1177 Reinhardt, Kurt F. "Evelyn Waugh: Christian Gentleman," *The Theological Novel of Modern Europe*. New York: F. Ungar, 1969. Pp. 203-216.

1178 "Requiem Mass, Mr. Evelyn Waugh," *Times*, 22 April 1966, p. 14.

1179 "Ritz-Carlton" [something on Waugh], *Bystander*, 30 January 1929, p. 212.

1180 Rolo, Charles. "Evelyn Waugh," *Critic*, 16 (May 1958), 11-13 and following.

1181 Rolo, Charles J. "Evelyn Waugh: The Best and the Worst," *Atlantic*, 194 (October 1954), 80, 82, 84-86.

1182 --- "Introduction," in Rolo (ed.), *The World of Evelyn Waugh*. Boston: Little, Brown, 1958. Pp. v-xvi. Revised version of *Atlantic* article.

1183 Roos, Hans-Dieter. "Die zwei Gesichter des Evelyn Waugh: Gespräch mit dem britischen Satiriker," *Die Kultur* (Munich), 7 (15 October 1958), 10.

1184 Rowse, A. L. *A Cornishman at Oxford*. London: Jonathan Cape, 1965. Pp. 24, 207.

1185 Russell, John. Editorial on Waugh, Hollis, Dawson, Maritain, and Roy Campbell, *Cherwell*, 6 May 1939, p. 24.

1187 Saltmarshe, Christopher. "Some Latter-Day 'Decadents,' "
     Bookman (London), 80 (1931), 196-197.

1188 "Salvete" [Waugh into Heads' Middle Four], *Lancing
     College Magazine*, May 1917, p. 58.

1189 Saunders, Hilary St. G. *Green Beret, The Story of the
     Commandoes, 1940-45.* London: M. Joseph, 1949.

1190 Savage, D. S. "The Innocence of Evelyn Waugh," in
     B. Rajan (ed.), *Focus Four: The Novelist as Thinker.*
     London: Dobson, 1947. Pp. 34-46. Also in *Western
     Review*, 14 (Spring 1950), 197-206.

1192 Schlüter, Kurt. "Evelyn Waugh," in Horst W. Drescher
     (ed.), *Englische Literatur der Gegenwart in
     Einzeldarstellungen.* Stuttgart: Kröner, 1970.
     Pp. 23-46.

1193 Schmid, Peter. "Evelyn Waugh, Beter und Spötter,"
     Weltwoche (Zurich), 16, No. 747 (5 March 1948), 5.

1194 "School Certificate" [Waugh gets his], *Lancing Col-
     lege Magazine*, November 1920, p. 82.

1195 "School Notes" [Waugh congratulated on being made a
     House Captain], *Lancing College Magazine*, June
     1921, p. 41.

1196 "School Notes" [Waugh as President of Debate Society
     is a "School Official"], *Lancing College Magazine*,
     November 1921, p. 81.

1197 Scargill, Laverna [probably Waugh]. "Correspondence"
     ["the Editor has left" - -after the relation of the hoax
     attack on his first editorial], *Lancing College Maga-
     zine*, March 1922, p. 31.

1198 "School Notes" [Waugh congratulated on winning Hert-
     ford Scholarship], *Lancing College Magazine*, Feb-
     ruary 1922, pp. 7-8.

1199 "School Notes" [Waugh has cartoon in *London Mercury*],
     Lancing College Magazine, July 1923, p. 100.

1200 Scientia Omnia Vincit. Letter to the Editor [on Debate
     Society closing], *Lancing College Magazine*, No-
     vember 1921, pp. 82-83.

1201 Seidler, Manfred. "Evelyn Waugh, Moralist und Satiriker,"
     Die Kirche in der Welt (Munster), VII (1954), 377-380.

1202 --- "Die ubergrossen und die kleinen Sunder: Über die
     Romane der englischen Konvertiten Graham Greene
     und Evelyn Waugh," *Werkhefte katholischer Laien*
     (Munich), 12 (1958), 234-239, 258-262.

1203 --- "Evelyn Waugh," in Rudolf Suhnel and Dieter
     Riesner (eds.), *Englische Dichter der Moderne: Ihr
     Leben und Werk*. Berlin: Erich Schmidt, 1971.

1204 Senile [probably Waugh]. An answer to E. W.'s Edito-
     rial, *Lancing College Magazine*, March 1922, p. 30.

1205 Servotte, Herman. "Evelyn Waugh 1903-1966: Vlucht in
     de komiek," *Dietsche Warande en Belfort*, 111 (1966),
     334-346.

1206 Sewell, Elizabeth. *The Field of Nonsense*. London:
     Chatto and Windus, 1952.

1207 "Shakespeare Society" [Waugh in "closed" society
     that read *Lear*], *Lancing College Magazine*, March
     1921, p. 20.

1208 "Shakespeare Society" [Waugh in "closed" society that
     read *Henry IV*, pt. II & *Macbeth*], *Lancing College
     Magazine*, July 1921, p. 60.

1209 "Shakespeare Society" [Waugh in "closed" society that
     read *A Midsummer Night's Dream*], *Lancing College
     Magazine*, November 1921, p. 77.

1210 "Shakespeare Society" [Waugh in "closed" society that read *The Winter's Tale*], *Lancing College Magazine*, December 1921, p.92.

1211 Sheehan, Edward. "Evelyn Waugh Runs a Fair," *Harper's*, 220 (January 1960), 30-37. Same as *Cornhill* article.

1212 --- "A Weekend with Waugh," *Cornhill Magazine*, 171 (Summer 1960), 209-225.

1213 Sheerin, J. B. "Waugh Appraises American Catholics," *Catholic World*, 170 (November 1949), 81-85.

1214 "Ship Evelyn Waugh's Library from London Via Lykes Lines," *Lykes Fleet Flashes*, November 1968, p. 4.

1215 Sitwell, Osbert. *Laughter in the Next Room*. Boston: Little, Brown, 1948.

1216 Smith, Lady Eleanor. "Bruno Hatte," *Sunday Dispatch*, 14 July 1929, p. 4.

1217 --- "Determined to Impress," *Sunday Dispatch*, 3 February 1929, p. 4.

1218 --- "Freemasonry among young authors, wise in publicity," *Sunday Dispatch*, 7 April 1929, p. 4.

1219 --- "From a Window in Vanity Fair," [on Mr. Wu], *Weekly Dispatch*, 13 March 1927, p. 5.

1220 --- "He is so" [E. Waugh helped Brian Howard with the Bruno Hat hoax], *Sunday Dispatch*, 28 July 1929, p. 4.

1221 --- "His Brother's Turn," *Weekly Dispatch*, 19 February 1928, p. 4.

1222 --- "Islington Home," *Sunday Dispatch* [*Weekly Dispatch* renamed], 23 September 1928, p. 4.

1223 --- "Mr. Rodd Instructs--At Last!" *Weekly Dispatch*, 1 April 1928, p. 4.

1224   --- "Tasting Power; Titular Legerdemain," *Sunday Dispatch*, 18 November 1928, p. 4.

1225   --- "Who Are They?" [characters in *Decline and Fall*], *Sunday Dispatch*, 23 September 1928, p. 4.

1226   Sobreira, Alberto. "Evelyn Waugh," *Brotéria: Revista contemporanea de cultura* (Lisbon), 82 (1966), 838-840.

1227   Soby, J. T. "Writer vs. Artist," *Saturday Review*, 29 (17 August 1946), 24-26.

1228   "Soccer Notes" [Heads' First League had good season; Waugh a "stalwart in the defense"], *Lancing College Magazine*, December 1921, pp. 88-91.

1229   Socrates. "A Night Out," *Isis*, 21 January 1965, pp. 13-14.

1230   Sonnenfeld, Albert. "Twentieth Century Gothic: Reflections on the Catholic Novel," *Southern Review*, NS 1 (April 1965), 388-405.

1231   Spender, Stephen. "The World of Evelyn Waugh," *The Creative Element: A Study of Vision, Despair and Orthodoxy among some Modern Writers*. London: Hamish Hamilton, 1953. Pp. 159-174; New York: British Book Center, 1954.

1231a   --- "Evelyn Waugh," one-hour taped lecture, McGraw-Hill Sound Seminar Series, No. 75915, 1968.

1232   Spiel, Hilde. "Enfant terrible des Katholizismus," *Der Park und die Wildnis: Zur Situation der neueren englischen Literatur*. Munich: Beck, 1953. Pp. 81-87.

1233   Staley, Thomas F. "Waugh the Artist," *Commonweal*, 84 (1966), 280-282.

1234 Stanford, Derek. *John Betjeman, A Study*. London: Neville Spearman, 1961.

1235 Stern, G. B. *Trumpet Voluntary*. New York: Macmillan, 1944. Pp. 272-276.

1236 Stevenson, Lionel. *The History of the English Novel*, Vol 11. New York: Barnes and Noble, 1967. Pp. 351-362 and *passim*.

1237 Stopes, Marie C. Letter to the Editor, "A Recent Novel," *Tablet*, 4 February 1933, p. 149. [Agrees with editor that *Black Mischief* is a sad novel].

1238 Stopp, Frederick J. "Apology and Expanation," *Renascence*, 10 (1957/58), 94-99.

1239 --- "The Circle and the Tangent," *Month*, 12 (July 1954), 18-34.

1240 --- "Das Groteske als Form der Wirklichkeitsdarstellung bei Greene und Waugh," *Jahres- und Tagungsbericht der Görres-Gesellschaft 1953*. Cologne: Buchemim Komm, 1954. Pp. 14-26.

1241 --- "Der katholische Roman im heutigen England: Graham Greene und Evelyn Waugh," *Stimmen der Zeit*, 153 (March 1954), 428-443.

1241a Stratford, Philip. "Man and Superman in the World of Waugh," *Parallel*, 1 (July-August 1967), 52-54.

1242 Straus, Ralph. "Evelyn Waugh" (Photo by J. Maycock), *Bystander*, 8 October 1930, p. 101.

1243 --- "Froth and First Novels," *Bystander*, 21 November 1928, p. v.

1244 Strong, L. A. G. *Green Memory*. London: Methuen, 1961.

1245 Stürzl, Erwin. "Evelyn Waughs Romanwerk: Makabre

Farce oder 'Menschliche Komödie'?'', *Die Neueren Sprachen*, 8 (1959), 314-326.

1246   "Success and Failure" [Robert Byron?], *Cherwell*, 14 November 1925, p. 103.

1247   Sutro, John [Uncle Julius], "The Railway Club" [Woodruff saying all roads lead to Rome], *Cherwell*, 21 June 1924, p. 191.

1248   "Swimming" [Waugh on Heads' team which was beaten by Gibbs' in first round of House matches, 26 May], *Lancing College Magazine*, June 1920, p. 36.

1249   Sykes, Christopher. "Evelyn," *Sunday Times*, 17 April 1966, p. 12.

1250   --- Evelyn Waugh--a brief life," *Listener*, 78 (24 August 1967), 225-229; also in Derwent May (ed.), *Good Talk*. London: Gollancz, 1968. Pp. 11-34.

1251   --- *Four Studies in Loyalty*. London: Collins, 1946.

1252   --- "The Pocket Waugh," *The Tablet*, 198 (7 July 1951), 9-10.

1253   ---, Cyril Connolly, Raymond Mortimer and Goronwy Rees. "A Critique of Waugh," *Listener*, 78 (31 August 1967), 267-269. Extracts from "Evelyn Waugh the Writer" broadcast in the B.B.C. Third Programme.

1254   Symons, Julian. "A Long Way from Firbank," *Critical Occasions*. London: Hamish Hamilton, 1966. Pp. 74-79.

1255   Talbot, Francis X., S. J. "Evelyn Waugh, Loyola Alumnus," *Evergreen Quarterly* (Loyola College, Baltimore), 4, No. 2 (Spring 1948), 24-30. Gives background of honorary doctorate awarded to Waugh, quotes from correspondence, and reproduces the last page of the corrected *Brideshead* proofs.

1256   Temple, Phillips. "Some Sidelights on Evelyn Waugh,"

America, 75 (27 April 1946), 75-76.

1257   Thérèse, Sister M. (ed.). "Waugh's Letters to Thomas
       Merton," *Evelyn Waugh Newsletter*, 3, i (Spring 1969) ,
       1-4.

1258   Tindall, William York. *Forces in Modern British Liter-
       ature, 1885-1956*. New York: Vintage Books, 1956.

1259   Todd, Olivier. "Evelyn Waugh ou le faux ennemi," *Temps
       modernes* (Paris), 8 (1953), 1406-1423.

1260   "Town and Country: Warwick Street," *Tablet*, 24 April
       1937, p. 608. [On Waugh's marriage.]

1261   "Town and Country," *Tablet*, 6 March 1937, p. 360.
       [Waugh a Chapman & Hall Director].

1262   Tracy, Honor. "Evelyn Revisited," *New Republic*, 158
       (23 March 1968), 39-41.

1263   Tree, Viola. "Ravishingly Beautiful," [on Mrs. Waugh],
       Sunday Dispatch, 6 October 1929, p. 4.

1264   --- [On the four Bright Young People], *Sunday Dispatch*,
       13 October 1929, p. 4.

1265   Tysdahl, Bjørn. "The Bright Young Things in the Early
       Novels of Evelyn Waugh," *Edda*, 62 (1962), 326-334.

1266   Ulanov, Barry. "The Ordeal of Evelyn Waugh," in
       Melvin J. Friedman, ed., *The Vision Obscured: Per-
       ceptions of Some Twentieth-Century Catholic Novel-
       ists*. New York: Fordham University Press, 1970, pp.
       79-93.

1267   Untitled. *Isis*, 21 January 1925, p. 13.

1268   Untitled. *Isis* Editor, editorial on Continental Travellers.
       Isis, 15 October 1924, p. 1.

1269 Untitled. [Probably Waugh]. Item on T. L. Greenidge's Banbury to Oxford race with photographs [Waugh paced him on a bicycle.] *Isis*, 6 February 1924, p. 5.

1270 Untitled. [Probably Waugh]. Item on Cruttwell's cricket. *Isis*, 24 May 1923, p. 6.

1271 Untitled. Article about the Hawthornden Prize, *Tablet*, 167 (27 June 1936), 828.

1272 Untitled. Biographical note, *Books on Trial*, 9 (October 1950), 123.

1273 "Valete." E. A. St. J. Waugh, Review of Lancing Career: Entered Heads' House, May 1917; House Captain, May 1921; Editor of Magazine, September 1921; President of L. C. D. S., September 1921; Librarian, May 1921; School Certificate, August 1920; Higher Certificate, August 1921; House Colours for Swimming; Lance Corporal in O. T. C.; Sixth form; History Scholarship to Hertford College, Oxford. *Lancing College Magazine*, February 1922, p. 11.

1274 Van Zeller, Dom Hubert. "An Appreciation of Evelyn Waugh," *Downside Review*, 84 (July 1966), 285-287.

1275 --- "Evelyn Waugh," *Month*, 36 (July-August, 1966), 69-71.

1276 Vice President, The [probably Waugh]. "The Union" column [on the cinema], *Isis*, 6 June 1923, p. 2.

1277 Von Puttkamer, Annemarie. "Evelyn Waugh," *Frankfurter Hefte*, 5 (1950), 869-872.

1278 Voorhees, Richard J. "Evelyn Waugh Revisited," *South Atlantic Quarterly*, 48 (April 1949), 270-280.

1279 Wagner, Geoffrey. *Wyndham Lewis; A Portrait of the Artist as the Enemy.* New Haven, Connecticut: Yale University Press, 1957.

1280   Wagner, Linda Welshimer. "Satiric Masks: Huxley and and Waugh," *Satire Newsletter*, 3, ii (Spring 1966), 160-162.

1281   Wall, Barbara. "Critics and Evelyn Waugh," *America*, 77 (28 June 1947), 354.

1282   Wall, Bernard. *Headlong into Change*. London: Collins, 1969.

1283   "Waugh on U. S. Catholicism," *America*, 81 (1 October 1949), 681.

1284   "Waugh Unmasked," *Jubilee*, 7 (October 1959), 43-45.

1285   "Waughisms: Evelyn Waugh's Article in *Life* on Catholic Church in the U. S. A.," *Ave Maria*, 70 (8 October 1949), 451.

1286   Waugh, Alec. *The Early Years of Alec Waugh*. London: Cassell, 1962.

1287   --- *In Praise of Wine, and Certain Noble Spirits*. New York: Sloane, 1959. Pp. 32, 62, 174-175.

1287a --- *Wines and Spirits*. New York: Time-Life Books, 1968. P. 100.

1288   --- "My Brother Evelyn," *Atlantic*, 219 (June 1967), 53-60.

1289   Waugh, Arthur. *One Man's Road, Being a Picture of Life in a Passing Generation*. London: Chapman and Hall, 1931.

1290   --- *One Hundred Years of Publishing, Being the Story of Chapman and Hall. Centenary, 1830-1930. By the Managing Director, 1901-1930*. London: Chapman and Hall, 1930.

1291   --- "Preface," *Tradition and Change*. London: Chapman and Hall, 1919. Pp. vii-viii.

1292 Waugh, Auberon. "Death in the Family," *Spectator*, 216 (6 May 1966), 562-563. See replies by Kenneth Allsop, John Davenport, and Marie-Louise Zulueta, *Spectator*, 216 (13 May 1966), 597-598, and Waugh's reply to Allott, 216 (20 May 1966), 630.

1293 Webster, Harvey Curtis. "Evelyn Waugh: Catholic Aristocrat," in *After the Trauma: Representative British Novelists Since 1920*. Lexington: The University Press of Kentucky, 1970. Pp. 72-92.

1293a Wells, Joel. "The Three Pigs by *v*l*n W**gh" in *Grim Fairy Tales for Adults*. New York: Macmillan, 1967. Pp. 31-35.

1294 --- "Why Two Members of the English Establishment Decided not to read Evelyn Waugh's Autobiography," *U. S. Catholic*, 30 (December 1964), 63 and following.

1294a West, Paul. *The Modern Novel*. Vol. 1, Revised edition. London: Hutchinson University Library, 1965. Pp. 66-68 and *passim*.

1295 West, Rebecca. "A Letter from Abroad," *Bookman* (New York), 71 (1930), 81-86. Under the title "Evelyn Waugh," in West, *Ending in Earnest: A Literary Log*. Garden City, New York: Doubleday, Doran, 1931. Pp. 217-226.

1296 Wheatley, George A. Letter to the Editor, *Spectator*, 216 (29 April 1966), 524.

1297 Earl of Wicklow [Lord Clonmore, or William Cecil James Howard]. "Evelyn Waugh--An Appreciation," *Irish Times*, 21 April 1966.

1298 --- *Fireside Fusilier*. Dublin: Clonmore and Reynolds, 1958.

1299   Wilson, Angus. Letter to the editor, *Spectator,* 216
         (29 April 1966), 524.

1300   Wilson, Colin. "Evelyn Waugh and Graham Greene,"
         *The Strength to Dream: Literature and the Imagin-
         ation.* Boston: Houghton, Mifflin, 1962. Pp. 42-55.
         Published as *Literature and the Imagination.* Lon-
         don: Gollancz, 1962.

1301   Wilson, Edmund. "Never apologize, never explain: The
         Art of Evelyn Waugh," and " Splendors and Miseries
         of Evelyn Waugh," *Classics and Commercials.* Lon-
         don: W. H. Allen, 1951. Pp. 140-146, 298-305. New
         York: Farrar, Straus and Co., 1950. Pp. 140-146,
         298-305.

1302   Woodcock, George. "Evelyn Waugh: The Man and His
         Work," *World Review,* 1 (March 1949), 51-56.

1303   Woodruff, Douglas. "Evelyn Waugh, the Man Behind the
         Writer," *Tablet,* 220 (16 April 1966), 441-442. Reply ,
         23 April 1966, p. 483.

1304   Woollcott, Alexander. *The Letters of Alexander Wollcott,*
         ed. by Beatrice Kaufman and Joseph Hennessey.
         New York: Viking, 1944. Pp. 392-393.

1305   "Wounded" (Waugh, Capt. E. A. St. J., Royal Horse
         Guards--Blues). *Lancing College Magazine,* Christ-
         mas Term, 1944, p. 133.

ARTICLES ON AND REVIEWS OF INDIVIDUAL WORKS

JUVENILIA

1306 "Library Notes," *Lancing College Magazine*, June 1919, p. 39.

1307 "The Library," *Lancing College Magazine*, April 1920, pp. 20-21.

1308 "Library Notes," *Lancing College Magazine*, February 1921, pp. 6-7.

1309 Del Re, Arundell. "The Oxford Arts Club," *Isis*, 20 June 1923, p. 12.

1310 Franklin, M. A. E. "Oxford Art Exhibition," *Isis*, 18 June 1924, pp. 18-19.

1311 Robot. "Arts Club Exhibition, A Little-Noticed Display," *Oxford Chronicle*, 20 June 1924, p. 16.

1312 M. A. S. Review of *Georgian Stories, 1926, Cherwell*, 13 November 1926, p. 155.

1313 Aiken, Conrad. *Literary Review*, 23 (9 April 1927), 4.

1314 R. R. *Cherwell*, 3 December 1932, p. 188.

THE SCARLET WOMAN

"The Scarlet Woman--An Ecclesiastical Melodrama" First shown Oxford University Dramatics Society. 22 November 1925.

THE SCARLET WOMAN con't.

Reviews

1315   Fernald, John. "Mr. Greenidge's Films," *Isis*, 2
       December 1925, p. 10.

1316   Greenidge, Terence. "The Cinematograph in Oxford,"
       Isis, 17 June 1925, p. 10.

1317   --- "The Story of Oxford Films," *Isis*, 24 November
       1926, p. 10. "Film Clips," *Sight and Sound* [London], 36 (Summer 1967), 154-155.

ROSSETTI: HIS LIFE AND WORKS

1318   Burra, Peter J. S. *Lancing College Magazine*, June,
       1928, pp. 89-90.

1319   Campbell, Roy. *Nation and Athenaeum*, 43 (19 May 1928),
       212.

1320   Craven, T. *Books* (New York Herald Tribune), 2 September 1928, p. 2.

1321   Lancaster, Osbert. *Isis*, 2 May 1928, p. 19.

1322   Lechlitner, Ruth. *New York Evening Post*, 4 August
       1928, p. 5.

1323   Meldrum, D. S. "Rossetti as Painter," *Bookman* (London), 74 (April 1928), 10-17.

1324   Quennell, Peter. *New Statesman*, 31 (12 May 1928),
       160.

1325   Shanks, Edward. "Dante Gabriel Rossetti," *London*

Mercury, 18 (May 1928), 67-78.

1326 Squire, J. C. *Observer,* 29 April 1928, p. 6.

1327 Taylor, Rachel A. "A King in Exile," *Spectator,* 140 (12 May 1928), 719-721.

1328 H. M. T. *Cherwell,* 16 June 1928, pp. 187-188.

1329 Whitridge, Arnold. *Saturday Review of Literature,* 5 (28 July 1928), 4.

1330 *Booklist,* 25 (December 1928), 117.

1331 *Boston Transcript,* 13 June 1928, p. 3.

1332 "Readers' Reports," *Life and Letters,* No. 2 (July 1928), pp. 141-142.

1333 *New York Times,* 24 June 1928, p. 5.

1334 *Saturday Review* (London), 145 (21 April 1928), 499.

1335 *Springfield Republican,* 20 May 1928, p. 76.

1336 "Dante Gabriel Rossetti," *Times Literary Supplement,* 10 May 1928, p. 341.

DECLINE AND FALL

1337 Bender, Elaine. "Sour Grapes," *Evelyn Waugh Newsletter,* 2 (Autumn 1968), 4-6.

1338 Doyle, Paul A. *"Decline and Fall:* Two Versions," *Evelyn Waugh Newsletter,* 1, ii (Autumn 1967), 4-5.

1339 Hollis, Christopher. "Introduction" to *Decline and Fall.*

DECLINE AND FALL con't.

London: Heinemann, 1966. The Modern Novel Series.

1340   Mace, Edward. "Waugh on the Floor," *The Observer Review*, 10 December 1967, p. 25. Account of filming of *Decline and Fall*.

1341   Willett, John. "How Well Have They Worn?--10: *Decline and Fall*," *Times*, 10 March 1966, p. 13.

Reviews

1342   Bennett, Arnold. "Books and Persons: Turning Over the Autumn Leaves. Defects in Book Lists for an Unusually Distinguished Season," *Evening Standard*, 11 October 1928, p. 5.

1343   Connolly, Cyril. "New Novels," *New Statesman*, 32 (3 November 1928), 126.

1344   Fleming, Peter. *Isis*, 17 October 1928, p. 11.

1345   J.M.S.G. *Cherwell*, 20 October 1928, p. 24.

1346   Gould, Gerald. "New Novels," *Observer*, 23 September 1928, p. 8.

1347   King, Richard. "With Silent Friends," *Tatler*, 7 November 1928, p. 266.

1348   F.M. *Daily Telegraph*, 14 September 1928, p. 6.

1349   Matthews, T. S. *New Republic*, 58 (17 April 1929), 259.

1350   Mortimer, Raymond. "New Novels," *Nation and Athenaeum*, 22 September 1928, p. 260.

1351   Ross, Mary. *Books* (New York Herald Tribune), 31 March 1929, p. 3.

1352   Straus, Ralph. "A Bystander Among the Books," *Bystander*, 21 October 1928, p. 260.

1353   *Boston Transcript*, 4 May 1929, p. 4.

1354   *Bookman* (London), 75 (October 1928), 59.

1355   *Life and Letters.* No. 7 (December 1928), 724-725.

1356   *Nation and Athenaeum*, 43 (22 September 1928), 796.

1357   *New York Times*, 7 April 1929, p. 6.

1358   *New York World*, 5 May 1929, p. 11.

1359   *Sign*, 22 (July 1943), 768.

1360   *Times Literary Supplement*, 27 September 1928, p. 685.

1361   *Times Literary Supplement*, 29 June 1962, p. 476.

1362   *Times Literary Supplement*, 24 August 1967, p. 759. (Hollis ed.)

VILE BODIES

1363   Isaacs, Neil D. "Evelyn Waugh's Restoration Jesuit," *Satire Newsletter*, 3 (Fall 1965), 91-94.

1364   Jervis, Steven A. "Evelyn Waugh, *Vile Bodies* and the Younger Generation," *South Atlantic Quarterly*, 66 (1967), 440-448.

1365   Kosok, Heinz. "The Film World of *Vile Bodies*," *Evelyn Waugh Newsletter*, 4 (Autumn 1970), 1-2.

1366   Linck, Charles E., and Robert Murray Davis. "The

VILE BODIES con't.

Bright Young People in *Vile Bodies,*" *Papers on Language and Literature*, 5 (1969), 80-90.

Reviews

1367   Aldington, Richard. "A Regionalist Novel," *Sunday Referee*, 9 February 1930, p. 6.

1368   Bennett, Arnold. "Books and Persons: Laughter--and a Lobster Supper; The Humorist Benefactor," *Evening Standard*, 30 January 1930, p. 9.

1369   Coxe, Howard. *New Republic*, 62 (7 May 1930), 333.

1370   Davenport, J. *Spectator*, 7 May 1965, p. 607.

1371   Ervine, St. John. "Do Our Publishers Really Know Their Job?" *Daily Express*, 30 January 1930, p. 6.

1372   Fitts, Dudley. *Nation*, 130 (21 May 1930), 602.

1373   Gould, Gerald. "Post-War and Pre-Waugh," *Observer*, 2 Feburary 1930, p. 8.

1374   Hartley. L. P. "New Fiction," *Saturday Review*, 149. (25 January 1930), 115.

1375   Linscott, R. W. *Books*, 16 March 1930, p. 7.

1376   Mais, S. P. B. "Fiction," *Daily Telegraph*, 17 January 1930, p. 15.

1377   Malcolm, A. E. C. "A Brilliant Book," *Cherwell*, 1 February 1930, pp. 31-32.

1378   Pritchett, V. S. "Fiction: Warnings," *Spectator*, 144 (18 January 1930), 99.

1379   Quennell, Peter. *Life and Letters*, 4 (February 1930), 246.

1380   E. S. "Current Literature: New Novels," *New States-man*, 8 February 1930, p. 572.

1381   Smith, Bernard. *New York World*, 13 July 1930, p. 7.

1382   Straus, Ralph. "Books and People: Mr. Evelyn Waugh Presents," *Bystander*, 15 January 1930, p. 140.

1383   Swinnerton, Frank. "A London Bookman's Week: Too Bogus," *Evening News*, 7 February 1930, p. 140.

1384   Wardman, Lawrence B. "A Subtler Michael Arlen," *New York Sun*, 21 March 1930, p. 32.

1385   Went, Stanley. *Saturday Review of Literature*, 6 (5 April 1930), 891.

1386   West, Rebecca. "A Study in Disillusionment," *Fortnightly Review*, 127 NS (February 1930), 273-274.

1387   "Novel Notes," *Bookman* (London), 77 (February 1930), 309.

1388   *Boston Transcript*, 3 May 1930, p. 8.

1389   "Books in Brief," *Nation and Anthenaeum*, 46 (15 February 1930), 682.

1390   *New Statesman*, 34 (8 February 1930), 572.

1391   *New York Times*, 23 March 1930, p. 7.

1392   *Times Literary Supplement*, 17 June 1965, p. 489.

LABELS (A BACHELOR ABROAD)

1393   Hobhouse, Chris. B. *Cherwell*, 8 November 1930, p. 101.

LABELS (A BACHELOR ABROAD) con't.

1394   Holt, Edgar. *Bookman* (London), 79 (November 1930), 140.

1395   Horgan, Paul. *Books*, 23 November 1930, p. 18.

1396   King, Richard. *Tattler*, 22 October 1930, p. 158.

1397   Lorentz, Pare. *New York Evening Post*, 29 November 1930, p. 46.

1398   Nicolson, Harold. *Daily Express*, 3 October 1930, p. 8.

1399   Segal, Mark. "Traveller's Toils," *Nation and Athenaeum*, 6 December 1930, p. 334.

1400   Straus, Ralph. "Labels and a Terrible Tale," *Bystander*, 1 October 1930, p. 48.

1401   *Nation*, 131 (3 December 1930), 630.

1402   "A Mediterranean Cruise," *New Statesman*, 36 (18 October 1930), 58-60.

1403   "Travelling for Pleasure," *Observer*, 12 October 1930, p. 7.

1404   *Saturday Review of Literature*, 7 (27 December 1930), 493.

1405   "Some More Books of the Week," *Spectator*, 145 (15 November 1930), 741-742.

1406   "A Mediterranean Journal," *Times Literary Supplement*, 23 October 1930, p. 863.

REMOTE PEOPLE (THEY WERE STILL DANCING)

1407   F. B. *Boston Transcript*, 2 January 1932, p. 1.

1408   Cowley, Malcolm. *New Republic*, 73 (16 November 1932), 22.

1409   Fleming, R. Peter. "Travellers," *Spectator*, 148 (23 January 1932), 118.

1410   Mears, Helen. *Survey*, 67 (1 March 1932), 634.

1411   Parkes, H. B. *Nation*, 134 (24 February 1932), 232.

1412   Swinnerton, Frank. "Travellers' Tales. Sometimes Without the Travel," *Evening News*, 30 October 1931, p. 11.

1413   West, Rebecca. "Picture of Travel Through Many Varied Lands, Pageant of the Near and Middle East," *Daily Telegraph*, 4 December 1931, p. 18.

1414   *Books*, 6 December 1931, p. 29.

1415   *Forum*, 87 (February 1932), xii.

1416   *New Republic*, 69 (23 December 1931), 169.

1417   *New York Times*, 3 January 1932, p. 8.

1418   "Africa and All That," *Observer*, 22 November 1931, p. 5.

1419   *Pittsburg, Monthly Bulletin*, 37 (June 1932), 37.

1420   *Saturday Review*, 152 (7 November 1931), 596.

1421   *Times Literary Supplement*, 5 November 1931, p. 864.

BLACK MISCHIEF

1422   Giraudou, Jean. Preface to *Diablerie,* French translation
        of *Black Mischief.* Paris: Grasset, 1938.

Reviews

1423   A. A. "New Novels," *Saturday Review,* 154 (1 October
        1932), 347.

1424   Agate, James. "Extravaganza," *Daily Express,* 6 Octob-
        er 1932, p. 6.

1425   Brande, Dorothea. *Bookman,* 75 (November 1932), 733.

1426   Cantwell, Robert. *Nation,* Vol. 135 (12 October 1932),
        p. 335.

1427   Chauveau, Paul. *Les Nouvelles Littéraires,* 19 March
        1938, p. 5.

1428   Cowley, Malcolm. *New Republic,* 73 (16 November 1932),
        22.

1429   A.E.M.G. *Cherwell,* 5 November 1933, pp. 91-92.

1430   Gould, Gerald. "White Mischief and Black," *Observer,*
        9 October 1932, p. 6.

1431   Linklater, Eric. "New Novels," *Listener,* 19 October
        1932, p. 576.

1432   Marshall, Howard. "Evelyn Waugh writes in a New
        Vein," *Daily Telegraph,* 4 October 1932, p. 16.

1433   Maxwell, William. *Books,* 9 October 1932, p. 7.

1434   Oldmeadow, Ernest. "New Books and Music--to Buy
        or Borrow or Leave Alone," *Tablet,* 7 January 1932,
        p. 10.

1435 --- "A Recent Novel," *Tablet*, 18 February 1933,
      pp. 213-215.

1436 Strong, Leonard A. G. "Fiction," *Spectator*, 149 (1
      October 1932), 420.

1437 *Boston Transcript*, 26 October 1932, p. 3.

1438 *Lancing College Magazine*, November 1932, p. 146.

1439 "Stories, Mostly Short," *New Statesman and Nation*,
      1 October 1932, p. 380.

1440 *New York Times*, 2 October 1932, p. 12.

1441 "New Books and Reprints," *Times Literary Supplement*,
      13 October 1932, p. 736.

NINETY TWO DAYS

1442 Armitage, Gilbert. *Bookman* (London), 86 (May 1934),
      121.

1443 T. C. *Commonweal*, 20 (1 June 1934), 137.

1444 Fleming Peter. *Spectator*, 152 (23 March 1934), 474-
      476.

1445 McCulloch, J. I. B.   *Saturday Review of Literature*,
      10 (23 June 1934), 769.

1446 Nils, Blair. *New York Times*, 27 May 1934, p. 12.

1447 Pritchett, V. S. *Christian Science Monitor*, 25 April
      1934, p. 10.

1448 Ruhl, Arthur. *Books*, 6 May 1934, p. 13.

NINETY TWO DAYS con't.

1449 *America*, 51 (14 July 1934), 333.

1450 *Booklist*, 30 (June 1934), 312.

1451 *Boston Transcript*, 23 May 1934, p. 3.

1452 *Cleveland Open Shelf*, July 1934, p. 15.

1453 *Extension*, 29 (July 1934), 52.

1454 "Central and South America," *Geographical Journal*, 84 (July-December 1934), 169-170.

1455 *Lancing College Magazine*, April 1934, p. 32.

1456 *New Republic*, 79 (6 June 1934), 109.

1457 *New Statesman and Nation*, 7 (17 March 1934), 420.

1458 *Times Literary Supplement*, 15 March 1934, p. 178.

A HANDFUL OF DUST

1459 Burbridge, Roger T. "The Function of Gossip, Rumor, and Public Opinion in Evelyn Waugh's *A Handful of Dust*," *Evelyn Waugh Newsletter*, 4, ii (Autumn 1970), 3-5.

1460 Cohen, Martin S. See entry under *Brideshead Revisited*.

1461 Davis, Robert Murray. "*Harper's Bazaar* and *A Handful of Dust*," *Philological Quarterly*, 48 (1969), 508-516.

1462 Green, Peter. "Du Côté de Chez Waugh," *Review of*

English Literature, 2 (1961), 89-100.

1463 Kearful, Frank J. "Tony Last and Ike McCaslin: The Loss of a Usable Past," *University of Windsor Review*, 3 (1968), ii, 45-52.

1464 Wasson, Richard. "*A Handful of Dust:* Critique of Victorianism," *Modern Fiction Studies*, 7 (1961/62), 327-337.

Reviews

1465 Agate, James. "Evelyn Waugh at His Best," *Daily Express*, 6 September 1934, p. 6.

1466 H.P.B. *Boston Transcript*, 17 October 1934, p. 3.

1467 Bergonzi, B. *Blackfriars*, 45 (July-August 1964), 349.

1468 Brophy, B. *New Statesman*, 68 (25 September 1964), 450.

1469 Chauveau, Paul. *Les Nouvelles Littéraires*, 24 May 1945, p. 3.

1470 Ellis, A. E. *Spectator*, 20 March 1964, p. 392.

1471 Holliday, Terence. *Books*, 23 September 1934, p. 10.

1472 Iles, Francis. "Destruction in Three Novels," *Daily Telegraph*, 7 September 1934, p. 7.

1473 Oldmeadow, Ernest. "The Pity of It," *Tablet*, 164 (8 September 1934), 300.

1474 Plomer, William. "Fiction," *Spectator*, 153 (14 September 1934), 374.

1475 Quennell, Peter. *New Statesman and Nation*, 8 (15 September 1934), 329.

1476 Sherman, Beatrice. *New York Times*, 30 September 1934, p. 7.

A HANDFUL OF DUST con't.

1477 Stewart, J. W. *Lancing College Magazine*, December 1934, p. 120.

1478 "Novels for the Library List," *Saturday Review*, 29 September 1934.

1479 *Times Literary Supplement*, 6 September 1934, p. 602.

1480 *Times Literary Supplement*, #3238 (5 March 1964), p. 201.

EDMUND CAMPION

1481 Maurois, Andre. Preface to the French translation of *Edmund Campion*. Chambéry: Amiot Dumont, 1953.

Reviews
First Edition

1482 M. A. *Lancing College Magazine*, December 1935, p. 136 .

1483 Burnham, Philip. *Commonweal*, 23 (27 December 1935), 247.

1484 Greene, Graham. *Spectator*, 155 (1 November 1935), 734-735.

1485 Hutchison, Percy. *New York Times*, 5 January 1936, p. 5 .

1486 T. P. *Boston Transcript*, 21 December 1935, p. 3.

1487 Quennell, Peter. *New Statesman and Nation*, 10 (28 September 1935), 422.

1488 *America*, 54 (28 December 1935), 283.

1489   *Blackfriars*, 17 (January 1935), 70.

1490   *Catholic Historical Review*, 22 (April 1936), 68.

1491   *Catholic World*, 143 (April 1936), 117.

1492   *Downside Review*, 53 (October 1935), 533.

1493   *G. K.'s Weekly*, 21 (19 September 1935), 450.

1494   *Homiletic and Pastoral Review*, 36 (July 1936), 1117.

1495   *Irish Ecclesiastical Record*, 46 (December 1935), 667.

1496   *Listener*, 13 November 1935, p. 887.

1497   *Month*, October 1935, pp. 377-378.

1498   *Pax*, 25 (December 1935), 213.

1499   *Studies*, 24 (December 1935), 686.

1500   *Times Literary Supplement*, 3 October 1935, p. 606.

Second Edition

1501   Etzhorn, L. R. *Library Journal*, 71 (15 June 1946), 918.

1502   Fremantle, Anne. *Weekly Book Review*, 21 July 1946,
         p. 12.

1503   Munn, L. S. *Springfield Republican*, 14 July 1946, p. 46.

1504   Rago, Henry. *Commonweal*, 44 (30 August 1946), 480-
         482.

1505   Redman, B. R. *Saturday Review*, 29 (13 July 1946), 11.

1506   M. S. *San Francisco Chronicle*, 15 September 1946, p. 15 .

1507   Sullivan, Richard. *New York Times*, 7 July 1946, p. 6.

EDMUND CAMPION con't.

1508   Wilson, Edmund. *New Yorker*, 22 (13 July 1946), 81.

1509   *America*, 75 (22 June 1946), 251.

1510   *Ave Maria*, 64 (19 October 1946), 506.

1511   *Best Sellers*, 6 (1 August 1946), 78.

1512   *Booklist*, 42 (1 July 1946), 347.

1513   *Catholic Historical Review*, 32 (January 1947), 436-438.

1514   *Extension*, 41 (September 1946), 30.

1515   *Kirkus*, 14 (15 April 1946), p. 191.

1516   *Sign*, 25 (July 1946), 53.

1517   *Time*, 68 (1 July 1946), 102.

1518   *Wisconsin Library Bulletin*, 42 (October 1946), p. 131.

Third Edition

1519   *Punch*, 27 September 1961, p. 481.

1520   *Tablet*, 216 (7 April 1962), 332.

1521   *Tablet*, 216 (5 May 1962), 434.

1522   Review of translation: Chaigne, Louis. *Les Nouvelles Littéraires*, 10 June 1954, p. 3.

MR. LOVEDAY'S LITTLE OUTING, AND OTHER SAD STORIES

1523   Barry, Iris. Mr. Loveday's Little Outing, and Other Sad Stories, *Books*, 1 November 1936, p. 12.

1524   Bowra, C. M. "Mr. Waugh's Short Stories," *Spectator*, 157 (10 July 1936), 70.

1525   Horder, J. P. *Lancing College Magazine*, July 1936, p. 76.

1526   Quennell, Peter. "New Novels," *New Statesman and Nation*, 12 (4 July 1936), 20.

1527   Walker-Smith, Derek. *English Review*, 63 (August 1936), 188-189.

1528   Walton, E. L. *New York Times*, 1 November 1936, p. 21.

1529   West, Douglas. *Daily Mail*, 2 July 1926, p. 6.

1530   *Saturday Review of Literature*, 15 (21 November 1936), 30.

1531   *Times Literary Supplement*, 4 July 1936, p. 561.

WAUGH IN ABYSSINIA

1532   Athill, Lawrence I. "The Ethiop Painted Black," *Spectator*, 13 November 1936, pp. 864-865.

1533   Attwater, Donald. *Dublin Review*, 200 (January-June 1937), 174-175.

1534   Bedoyere, Count Michael de la. *Catholic Herald*,

WAUGH IN ABYSSINIA con't.

31 October 1936, p. 3.

1535 Froshaug, E. P. C. *Lancing College Magazine*, December 1936, p. 117.

1536 Garnett, David. *New Statesman and Nation*, 12 (7 November 1936), 735.

1537 Stone, Geoffrey. *American Review*, 9 (April 1937), 114.

1538 *Foreign Affairs*, 15 (July 1937), 770.

1539 *G. K.'s Weekly*, 24 (5 November 1936), 172.

1540 *New York Times*, 13 June 1937, p. 11.

1541 *Spectator*, 157 (13 November 1936), 864.

1542 "Light in a Dark Place," *Tablet*, 168 (14 November 1936), 672.

1543 *Times Literary Supplement*, 7 November 1936, p. 900.

SCOOP

1544 Davis, Robert Murray. "Some Textual Variants in *Scoop,*" *Evelyn Waugh Newsletter*, 1 (Autumn 1967), 1-3.

Reviews

1545 Bradbury, Malcolm. *Spectator*, #7042 (11 September 1964), p. 347.

1546 Brophy, B. *New Statesman*, 68 (25 September 1964), 450.

A Checklist

1547   Burdett, Francis. "Fiction," *Catholic Herald*, 27 May
       1938, p. 4.

1548   Bush, G. *Lancing College Magazine*, June 1938,
       p. 56.

1549   Fadiman, Clifton. "Messrs Sheehan, Waugh, McIntyre,"
       New Yorker, 14 (23 July 1938), 56.

1550   Ferguson, Otis. "Action Stuff," *New Republic*, 95 (27
       July 1938), 340.

1551   Holliday, Terence. "Buggy Ride for the War Correspon-
       dents," *Saturday Review of Literature*, 18 (16 July
       1938), 7.

1552   Lazare, Christopher. *Nation*, 147 (3 September 1938),
       229.

1553   Pritchett, V. S. *Christian Science Monitor*, 15 June
       1938, p. 11.

1554   Shawe-Taylor, Desmond. *New Statesman and Nation*,
       15 (7 May 1938), 795.

1555   Soskin, William. *Books*, 17 July 1938, p. 2.

1556   Tourtellot, A. B. *Boston Transcript*, 6 August 1938,
       p. 1.

1557   Verschoyle, Derek. "Introducing the Boots," *Spectator*,
       160 (13 May 1938), 886.

1558   A. S. W. *Manchester Guardian*, 17 May 1938, p. 7.

1559   *America*, 59 (27 August 1938), 501.

1560   *Booklist*, 35 (1 September 1938), 10.

1561   *Catholic World*, 148 (October 1938), 122.

SCOOP con't.

1562 *Extension*, 33 (October 1938), 52.

1563 *Sign*, 18 (September 1938), 122.

1564 *Springfield Republican*, 11 September 1938, p. 7.

1565 *Tablet*, 171 (7 May 1938), 606.

1566 "Wrong Boot," *Time*, 32 (18 July 1938), 48-50.

1567 *Times Literary Supplement*, 7 May 1938, p. 313.

1568 *Times Literary Supplement*, (10 September 1964), p. 837.

1569 *Weekly Review*, 27 (19 May 1938), 196.

ROBBERY UNDER LAW (MEXICO: AN OBJECT LESSON)

1570 Gower, William. *Spectator*, 21 July 1939, p. 103.

1571 A.W.J. *Manchester Guardian*, 28 July 1939, p. 7.

1572 James, E. K. *Living Age*, 357 (October 1939), 197.

1573 Magner, J. A. *Commonweal*, 31 (24 November 1939), 120.

1574 Martin, R. L. *New York Times*, 19 November 1939, p. 9.

1575 McS., J. *Catholic World*, 150 (October 1939), 120.

1576 Parkes, H. B. *Books*, 24 September 1939, p. 9.

1577 Vann, Gerald. *Dublin Review*, 205 (June-December 1939), 443-445.

1578   *America,* 62 (4 November 1939), 106-107.

1579   *Catholic Historical Review,* 27 (April 1941), 139.

1580   *Columbia,* 19 (November 1939), 14.

1581   *Month,* 174 (August 1939), 146-154.

1582   *New Yorker,* Vol. 15 (23 September 1939), p. 79.

1583   *Tablet,* 174 (1 July 1939), 15-16.

1584   *Times Literary Supplement,* 1 July 1939, p. 103.

PUT OUT MORE FLAGS

1585   Abrahams, William. *Boston Globe,* 20 May 1942, p. 15.

1586   Bower, Anthony. *Nation,* 154 (6 June 1942), 658.

1587   Cerf, B. A. *Books,* 24 May 1942, p. 5.

1588   Corpse [C. L. Chamberlain]. *Lancing College Magazine,*
         Summer Term, 1942, p. 103.

1589   Dangerfield, George. *Saturday Review of Literature,*
         25 (30 May 1942), 7.

1590   Gay, R. M. *Atlantic,* 170 (September 1942), 140.

1591   Jack, P. M. *New York Times,* 7 June 1942, p. 7.

1592   Marlowe, Jack. *Penguin New Writing,* 14 (September 1942),
         133-140.

1593   Marriot, Charles. *Manchester Guardian,* 25 March 1942,
         p. 3.

PUT OUT MORE FLAGS con't.

1594   O'Brien, Kate. *Spectator*, 168 (3 April 1942), 336.

1595   Pryce-Jones, Alan. *New Statesman and Nation*, 23 (11 April 1942), 245.

1596   Thompson, Dunstan. *New Republic*, 107 (13 July 1942), 60.

1597   E. W. *Times Literary Supplement*, 24 August 1967, p. 759.

1598   Wright, Cuthbert. *Commonweal*, 36 (12 June 1942), 185.

1599   *Best Sellers*, 2 (27 May 1942), 55-56.

1600   *Catholic World*, 155 (June 1942), 381.

1601   *New Yorker*, 18 (30 May 1942), 66.

1602   *Pratt*, October 1942, p. 13.

1603   *Sign*, 22 (December 1942), 273.

1604   *Time*, 39 (25 May 1942), 90.

1605   *Times Literary Supplement*, 21 March 1942, p. 137.

BRIDESHEAD REVISITED

1606   Beary, Thomas John. "Religion and the Modern Novel," *Catholic World*, 166 (December 1947), 203-211.

1607   Beeger, Susanne. "Die englische Gesellschaft zwischen den Kriegen," *Die Neueren Sprachen*, NS 1 (1952), 244-257.

1608   Churchill, Thomas. "The Trouble with *Brideshead Re-visited*," *Modern Language Quarterly*, 28 (1967), 213-228.

1609   Clodd, Alan. "Some Textual Variants in *Brideshead*," *Evelyn Waugh Newsletter*, 3, i (Spring 1969), 5-6.

1610   Cogley, John. "Revisiting Brideshead," *Commonweal*, 80 (1964), 103-106.

1611   Cohen, Martin S. "Allusive Conversation in *A Handful of Dust* and *Brideshead Revisited*," *Evelyn Waugh Newsletter*, 5 (Autumn 1971), 1-6.

1612   Davis, Robert Murray. "Notes Toward a Variorum *Brideshead*," *Evelyn Waugh Newsletter*, 2, iii (Winter 1968), 4-6.

1613   --- "The Serial version of *Brideshead Revisited*," *Twentieth Century Literature*, 15 (1969), 35-43.

1614   Delasanta, Rodney, and Mario L. D'Avanzo. "Truth and Beauty in *Brideshead Revisited*," *Modern Fiction Studies*, 11 (1965/66), 140-152.

1615   Doyle, Paul A. "*Brideshead* Rewritten," *Catholic Book Reporter*, 2 (April-May 1962), 9-10.

1616   --- "Waugh's *Brideshead Revisited*," *Explicator*, 24 (March 1966), item 57.

1617   Hardy, John Edward. "*Brideshead Revisited*: God, Man, and Others," *Man in the Modern Novel*. Seattle: University of Washington Press, 1964. Pp. 159-174.

1618   Harty, E. R. "*Brideshead* Re-read: A Discussion of Some of the Themes of Evelyn Waugh's *Brideshead Revisited*," *Unisa English Studies*, 3 (1967), 66-74.

1619   Heilman, Robert B. "Sue *Bridehead Revisited*," *Accent*, 7 (1946/47), 123-126.

BRIDESHEAD REVISITED con't.

1620 Kahrmann, Bernd. *Die idyllische Szene im zeitgenössichen englischen Roman, Linguistica et Litteraria* (Bad Homburg, Berlin Zurich, 1969), pp. 62-65.

1621 Kosok, Heinz. "Evelyn Waugh: *Brideshead Revisited,*" in Horst Oppel (ed.), *Der moderne englische Roman: Interpretationen.* Berlin: Erich Schmidt, 1965. Pp. 301-327. Revised edition, 1971. Pp. 302-329.

1622 LaFrance, Marston. "Context and Structure of Evelyn Waugh's *Brideshead Revisited,*" *Twentieth Century Literature,* 10 (1964), 12-18.

1623 Martindale, C. C. "Back again to 'Brideshead,' " *Twentieth Century,* 2 (1948), 26-33.

1624 Phillips, Gene D. "The Page Proofs of *Brideshead Revisited,*" *Evelyn Waugh Newsletter,* 5 (Autumn 1971), 7-8.

1625 Stopp, Frederick J. "Grace in Reins: Reflections on Mr. Waugh's *Brideshead* and *Helena,*" *Month,* 10 (August 1953), 69-84.

1626 Szala, Alina. *"Brideshead Revisited* Evelyna Waugh," *Roczniki Humanistyczne,* 6 (1957), vi, 95-105; English summary 156-157.

1627 Vredenburgh, Hoseph. "The Character of the Incest Object: A Study of Alternation between Narcissism and Object Choice," *American Imago,* 14 (1957), 45-52.

1628 Wooton, Carl. "Evelyn Waugh's *Brideshead Revisited:* War and Limited Hope," *Midwest Quarterly,* 10 1969), 359-375.

Reviews

1629 Beresford, J. D. *Manchester Guardian*, 1 June 1945, p. 3 .

1630 Chilton, E. E. *Saturday Review of Literature*, 29 (5 January 1946), 6.

1631 Clinton-Baddeley, V. C. *Spectator*, 174 (8 June 1945), 532.

1632 Fremantle, Anne. *Commonweal*, 43 (4 January 1946), 311 .

1633 Gardiner, H. "Waugh's Away Critics: Brideshead Baffles the Bookmen," *America*, 74 (12 January 1946), 409-410.

1634 Garrison, W. E. *Christian Century*, 63 (24 April 1946), 527.

1635 Hutchens, J. K. *New York Times*, 30 December 1945, p. 1.

1636 Lalou, Rene. *Les Nouvelles Littéraires*, 29 May 1947.

1637 Lewis, E. L. *Library Journal*, 71 (1 January 1946), 96.

1638 McSorley, Joseph. *Catholic World*, 162 (February 1946), 469.

1639 Munn, L. S. *Springfield Republican*, 13 January 1946, p. 46.

1640 Prescott, Orville. *Yale Review*, 35 (Spring 1946), 573.

1641 Reed, Henry. *New Statesman and Nation*, 29 (23 June 1945), 408.

1642 Spectorsky, A. C. *Book Week*, 30 December 1945, p. 1.

1643 Sugrue, Thomas. *Weekly Book Review*, 6 January 1946, p. 1.

BRIDESHEAD reviews con't.

1644   Trilling, Diana. *Nation*, 162 (5 January 1946), 20.

1645   Weeks, Edward. *Atlantic*, 177 (January 1946), 151.

1646   Wilson, Edmund. *New Yorker*, 21 (5 January 1946), 71.

1647   *America*, 74 (12 January 1946), 411.

1648   *Ave Maria*, 63 (2 March 1946), 283.

1649   *Best Sellers*, 5 (1 February 1946), 197-198.

1650   *Booklist*, 42 (1 January 1946), 150.

1651   *Catholic World*, 162 (February 1946), 197-198.

1652   *Cleveland Open Shelf*, January 1946, p. 4.

1653   *Columbia*, 25 (May 1946), 13.

1654   *Commonweal*, 43 (4 June 1946), 311-313.

1655   *Dominicana*, 31 (March 1946), 283.

1656   *Irish Monthly*, 76 (June 1948), 260-264.

1657   *Kirkus*, 13 (1 November 1945), 475.

1658   *Sign*, 25 (February 1946), 469-470.

1659   *Time*, 47 (7 January 1946), 411.

1660   *Times Literary Supplement*, 2 June 1945, p. 257.

1661   *Wisconsin Library Bulletin*, 42 (March 1946), 47.

Reviews of Revised Edition

1662 Coleman, John. *Spectator*, 29 July 1960, p. 187.

1663 Kermode, Frank. *Encounter*, November 1960, p. 63.

1664 Pryce-Jones, David. "The Social Philistine," *Time and Tide*, 41 (23 July 1960), 863-864.

1665 *Punch*, 3 August 1960, p. 177.

1666 *Times Literary Supplement*, 16 September 1960, p. 594.

WHEN THE GOING WAS GOOD

1667 Connolly, F. X. *Commonweal*, 45 (24 January 1947), 376.

1668 Fleming, Peter. *Spectator*, 178 (24 January 1947), 116.

1669 Forbes-Boyd, Eric. *Christian Science Monitor*, 21 February 1947, p. 20.

1670 Sugrue, Thomas. *New York Herald Tribune Weekly Book Review*, 5 January 1947, p. 4.

1671 Watts, Richard. *New York Times*, 12 January 1947, p. 7.

1672 Willis, K. T. *Library Journal*, 72 (15 January 1947), 160.

1673 Woodburn, John. *Saturday Review*, 30 (1 February 1947), 12.

1674 *Best Sellers*, 6 (15 February 1947), 189.

1675 *Catholic World*, 164 (March 1947), 573.

1676 *Columbia*, 45 (February 1947), 13.

WHEN THE GOING WAS GOOD con't.

1677 *Kirkus*, 14 (15 November 1946), 585.

1678 *New Yorker*, 22 (11 January 1947), 85.

1679 *Sign*, 26 (February 1947), 54.

1680 *Springfield Union*, 25 June 1947, p. 2.

1681 *Time*, 49 (13 January 1947), 104.

SCOTT KING'S MODERN EUROPE

1682 Brighouse, Harold. *Manchester Guardian*, 2 January 1948, p. 3.

1683 Broderick, John. *New Yorker*, 25 (5 March 1949), 89.

1684 Cousins, Norman. *Saturday Review*, 32 (26 February 1949), 12.

1685 Dedmon, Emmett. *Chicago Sun*, 20 February 1949, p. 8.

1686 Evans, Ernestine. *Commonweal*, 49 (18 March 1949), 571.

1687 W. H. H. *Springfield Republican*, 20 February 1949, p. 22A.

1688 Jackson, J. H. *San Francisco Chronicle*, 4 March 1949, p. 16.

1689 King, Robin. *Spectator*, 180 (9 January 1948), 52.

1690 Orwell, George. *New York Times*, 20 February 1949, p. 1.

1691   Rolo, C. J. *Atlantic*, 183 (March 1949), 85.

1692   Strachey, Julia. *New Statesman and Nation*, 35 (31 January 1948), 98.

1693   Sutcliffe, Denham. *Christian Science Monitor*, 24 February 1949, p. 11.

1694   Whicher, G. F. *New York Herald Tribune Weekly Book Review*, 20 February 1949, p. 10.

1695   Willis, K. T. *Library Journal*, 74 (15 February 1949), 314.

1696   Woodburn, John. *New Republic*, 120 (21 March 1949), 23.

1697   *Blackfriars*, 29 (February 1948), 107.

1698   *Booklist*, 45 (15 February 1949), 211.

1699   *Catholic World*, 168 (March 1949), 495.

1700   *Kirkus*, 17 (15 January 1949), 33.

1701   *Tablet*, 191 (24 January 1948), 58.

1702   *Time*, 53 (21 February 1949), 110.

THE LOVED ONE

1703   Bayley, John. "Two Catholic Novelists," *National Review*, 132 (February 1949), 232-235. See reply by Neill and Johnston, "The Catholic Novelists."

1704   Connolly, Cyril. "Introduction to *The Loved One*," *Horizon*, 17 (1948), 76-77.

THE LOVED ONE con't.

1705 Eichelbaum, S. "The Loved One Revisited," *Ramparts*, 3 (March 1965), 7-8 *passim*.

1706 MacShane, Frank. "Forest Lawn," *Prairie Schooner*, 35 (1961), 137-148.

1707 Neill, D. G., and F. C. Johnston. "The Catholic Novelists," *National Review*, 132 (1949), 345. Reply to Bayley.

1708 Powell, Dilys. "Death sans Sting," review of film, *The Loved One*, *Sunday Times*, 3 April 1966.

1709 Powers, J. F. "Waugh Out West," *Commonweal*, 48 (1948), 326-327.

1710 Prouse, Derek. Interview with Tony Richardson, director of film version of *The Loved One*, *Sunday Times*, 13 February 1966, p. 28.

1711 Ryan, H. F. "Vista of Diminished Truth: *The Loved One*," *America*, 82 (12 November 1949), 157-158.

1712 Spoerri, Erika. "Der Tod in Hollywood: Zu Evelyn Waughs neuem Roman," *Universitas*, 5 (1950), 1529-1531.

1713 Stone, Linton. "Introduction" to *The Loved One*. London: Heinemann, 1967. The Modern Novel Series.

1714 Wecter, Dixon. "On Dying in Southern California," *Pacific Spectator*, 2 (1948), 375-387.

Reviews

1715 Barry, Iris. *New York Herald Tribune Weekly Book Review*, 27 June 1948, p. 4.

1716 Bregy, Katherine. *Catholic World*, 167 (September 1948), 570.

1717 Cooke, Alistair. *Manchester Guardian*, 19 November 1948, p. 3.

1718 Davenport, John. *Spectator*, 7 May 1965, p. 607.

1719 Dedmon, Emmett. *Chicago Sun*, 4 July 1948, p. 6.

1720 Gibbs, Wolcott. *New Yorker*, 24 (26 June 1948), 71.

1721 Graham, W. S. *New Republic*, 18 (26 April 1948), 28.

1722 Jackson, J. H. *San Francisco Chronicle*, 22 June 1948, p. 18.

1723 Jones, Ernest. *Nation*, 167 (31 July 1948), 132.

1724 Kennedy, J. S. *Catholic World*, 168 (December 1948), 212.

1725 Kingery, R. E. *Library Journal*, 73 (15 June 1948), 946.

1726 Lalou, Rene. *Les Nouvelles Littéraires*, 29 September 1949.

1727 Lee, Robert. *Spectator*, 180 (5 March 1948), 296.

1728 Morris, A. S. *New York Times*, 27 June 1948, p. 1.

1729 Petersen, C. *Books Today*, 3 (27 February 1966), 13.

1730 Prescott, Orville. *Yale Review*, 38 (Autumn 1948), 190.

1731 Redman, B. R. *Saturday Review*, 31 (26 June 1948), 9.

1732 Rolo, C. J. *Atlantic*, 182 (July 1948), 104.

1733 Smith, R. D. *New Statesman and Nation*, 36 (11 December 1948), 528.

1734 Woodburn, John. *New Republic*, 119 (26 July 1948), 24.

THE LOVED ONE reviews con't.

1735 *Booklist*, 44 (1 July 1948), 368.

1736 *Kirkus*, 16 (1 May 1948), 220.

1737 *Time*, 52 (12 July 1948), 86.

1738 *Times Literary Supplement*, 20 November 1948, p. 652.

1739 *Times Literary Supplement*, 17 June 1965, p. 489.

HELENA

1740 Allen, W. G. "Evelyn Waugh's *Helena*," *Irish Monthly*, 79 (February 1951), 96-97.

1741 Dever, Joe. "Echoes of Two Waughs," *Commonweal*, 50 (1950), 68-70.

1742 Joost, Nicholas. "Waugh's *Helena*, Chapter VI," *Explicator*, 9 (April 1951), item 43.

1743 Menen, Aubrey. "The Baroque and Mr. Waugh," *Month*, 5 (April 1951), 226-237.

1744 Stopp, Frederick J. "Grace in Reins: Reflections on Mr. Waugh's *Brideshead* and *Helena*," *Month*, 10 (August 1953), 69-84.

Reviews

1745 Allen, W. G. *Irish Monthly*, 79 (February 1951), 96-97.

1746 Belvedere, J. *Best Sellers*, 10 (1 November 1950), 128.

1747 Charques, R. D. *Spectator*, 184 (13 October 1950), 388.

1748   Fausset, H. *Manchester Guardian*, 13 October 1950, p. 4.

1749   Gardiner, H. C. *America*, 84 (11 November 1950), 170.

1750   Gaul, C. C. *Christian Century*, 67 (1 November 1950), 1297.

1751   Henderson, R. W. *Library Journal*, 75 (15 October 1950), 1825.

1752   Paulding, Gouverneur. *New York Herald Tribune Book Review*, 22 October 1950, p. 6.

1753   Raymond, John. *New Statesman and Nation*, 40 (21 October 1950), 374.

1754   Rolo, C. J. *Atlantic*, 186 (November 1950), 98.

1755   Rovere, R. H. *New Yorker*, 26 (21 October 1950), 130.

1756   Smith, Bradford. *Saturday Review*, 33 (21 October 1950), 17.

1757   Sullivan, Richard. *Chicago Sunday Tribune*, 15 October 1950, p. 3.

1758   Sylvester, Harry. *New York Times*, 15 October 1950, p. 4.

1759   White, W. R. *San Francisco Chronicle*, 5 November 1950, p. 19.

1760   *Booklist*, 47 (15 November 1950), 116.

1761   *Christian Science Monitor*, 21 October 1950, p. 10.

1762   *Kirkus*, 18 (15 August 1950), 486.

1763   *New Republic*, 123 (18 December 1950), 23.

1764   *Springfield Republican*, 26 November 1950, p. 8.

HELENA reviews con't.

1765   *Time,* 56 (23 October 1950), 106.

1767   *Times Literary Supplement,* 13 October 1950, p. 641.

1768   *Wisconsin Library Bulletin,* 46 (November 1950), 19.

MEN AT ARMS

[Articles on the three novels of the war trilogy are gathered under the SWORD OF HONOUR listing.]

1769   Belvedere, J. *Best Sellers,* 12 (1 November 1952), 164.

1770   Connolly, Francis X. *America,* 88 (1 November 1952), 132-133.

1771   Fitzgerald, D. *Tablet,* 200 (13 September 1952), 211.

1772   Frank, Joseph. *New Republic,* 127 (10 November 1952), 19.

1773   Gray, James. *Saturday Review,* 35 (25 October 1952), 22.

1774   Hilton, James. *New York Herald Tribune Book Review,* 19 October 1952, p. 1.

1775   Hughes, Riley. *Catholic World,* 176 (December 1952), 232.

1776   Hughes, Serge. *Commonweal,* 57 (24 October 1952), 78-79.

1777   Jackson, J. H. *San Francisco Chronicle,* 31 October 1952, p. 21.

1778   Joost, N. *Books on Trial,* 11 (November 1952), 54.

1779   Knox, R. *Month*, 8 (October 1952), 236-238.

1780   Lalou, Rene. *Les Nouvelles Littéraires*, 11 March 1954.

1781   Lean, Tangye. *Spectator*, 189 (12 September 1952), 342.

1782   Morris, Alice. *New York Times*, 19 October 1952, p. 5.

1783   Pickrel, Paul. *Yale Review*, 42 (Winter 1953), 12.

1784   Raymond, John. *New Statesman and Nation*, 44 (20 September 1952), 326.

1785   Schwartz, Delmore. *Partisan Review*, 19 (1952), 703-704.

1786   Schwinn, L. *American Benedictine Review*, 3 (Winter 1952), 366.

1787   Shepperd, L. C. *Books on Trial*, 11 (November 1952), 73.

1788   Shrapnel, Norman. *Manchester Guardian*, 12 September 1952, p. 4.

1789   Slade, L. *Sign*, 32 (November 1952), 65-66.

1790   Stack, K. G. *Extension*, 47 (December 1952), 34.

1791   Sullivan, Richard. *Chicago Sunday Tribune*, 19 October 1952, p. 5.

1792   Weeks, Edward. *Atlantic*, 190 (December 1952), p. 88.

1793   Zipprich, M. H. *Library Journal*, 77 (1 October 1952), p. 1657.

1794   *Ave Maria*, 82 (3 September 1955), 23.

1795   *Dominicana*, 38 (March 1953), 48-49.

1797   *Kirkus*, 20 (1 September 1952), 569.

MEN AT ARMS con't.

1798   *New Yorker*, 28 (1 November 1952), 129.

1799   *Newsweek*, 40 (20 October 1952), 51.

1800   *Time*, 60 (27 October 1952), 104, 106.

1801   *Times Literary Supplement*, 12 September 1952, p. 593.

THE HOLY PLACES

1802   Fremantle, A. *Commonweal*, 59 (26 February 1954), 538.

1803   Martindale, C. *Month*, 9 (May 1953), 316.

1804   Moriarty, F. *America*, 90 (20 March 1954), 658.

1805   Thompson, B. *Catholic World*, 179 (May 1954), 158.

1806   Willmering, H. *Books on Trial*, 12 (March 1954), 199.

1807   *Tablet*, 201 (7 February 1953), 110-111.

LOVE AMONG THE RUINS

1808   Cosman, Max. *Arizona Quarterly*, 10 (Summer 1954), 169-172.

1809   Hollis, Christopher. *Tablet*, 201 (27 June 1953), 563.

1810   Pick, John. *Renascence*, 7 (Autumn 1954), 39.

1811   *Month*, 10 (August 1953), 123.

TACTICAL EXERCISE

1812   Barr, Donald. *New York Times*, 17 October 1954, p. 6.

1813   Coxe, L. O. *New Republic*, 131 (8 November 1954), 20.

1814   Gardiner, H. *America*, 92 (16 October 1954), 76.

1815   Hughes, Riley. *Catholic World*, 180 (November 1954), 151.

1816   Maloney, J. *Best Sellers*, 14 (1 November 1954), 121.

1817   O'Connor, Frank. *New York Herald Tribune Book Review*, 7 November 1954, p. 10.

1818   Pickrel, Paul. *Yale Review*, 44 (Winter 1955), 319.

1819   Pusateri, L. *Sign*, 34 (December 1954), 62.

1820   Quinn, P. F. *Commonweal*, 61 (12 November 1954), 171.

1821   Reynolds, Horace. *Saturday Review*, 37 (16 September 1954), 17.

1822   Steggert, F. *Books on Trial*, 13 (November 1954), 73.

1823   Sullivan, Richard. *Chicago Sunday Tribune*, 21 November 1954, p. 6.

1824   Walbridge, E. F. *Library Journal*, 79 (1 November 1954), 2104.

1825   Walsh, J. *Today*, 10 (February 1955), 20.

TACTICAL EXERCISE con't.

1826   White, W. R. *San Francisco Chronicle*, 31 October 1954, p. 18.

1827   *Booklist*, 51 (15 November 1954), 134.

1828   *Kirkus*, 22 (1 August 1954), 501.

OFFICERS AND GENTLEMEN

1829   Amis, Kingsley. *Spectator*, 8 July 1955, p. 56.

1830   Bradford, Curtis. *New Republic*, 133 (11 July 1955), 1494.

1831   Cooperman, Stanley. *Nation*, 181 (10 September 1955), 230.

1832   Cotter, J. *Sign*, 35 (September 1955), 63.

1833   Coxe, L. O. *Yale Review*, 45 (Autumn), 159.

1834   Cuneo, P. *Books on Trial*, 14 (September 1955), 11.

1835   Fitzgerald, D. *Tablet*, 206 (2 July 1955), 14.

1836   Gardiner, H. *America*, 93 (13 August 1955), 475.

1837   Gray, James. *Saturday Review*, 38 (9 July 1955), 10.

1838   Hass, V. P. *Chicago Sunday Tribune* (17 July 1955), 476.

1839   Horchler, R. T. *Commonweal*, 62 (12 August 1955), 476.

1840   Hughes, Riley. *Catholic World*, 181 (September 1955), 471.

1841   Lalou, Rene. *Les Nouvelles Littéraires*, 31 May 1956.

1842   Lindley, R. *Month*, 14 (September 1955), 182.

1843   McLaughlin, Richard. *Springfield Republican*, 14 August 1955, p. 4c.

1844   Moore, Geoffrey. *New York Times*, 10 July 1955, p. 50.

1845   O'Gorman, F. *Best Sellers*, 15 (1 August 1955), 79.

1846   Richardson, Maurice. *New Statesman and Nation*, 50 (9 July 1955), 50.

1847   Rolo, C. J. *Atlantic*, 196 (August 1955), 84.

1848   Shrapnel, Norman. *Manchester Guardian*, 1 July 1955, p. 4.

1849   Sullivan, Richard. *New York Herald Tribune Book Review*, 10 July 1955, p. 1.

1850   Sykes, Christopher. "Forward to Victory," *Time and Tide*, 36 (2 July 1955), 871-872.

1851   White, W. R. *San Francisco Chronicle*, 28 July 1955, 19.

1852   *Christian Century*, 72 (24 August 1955), 973.

1853   *Dominicana*, 40 (December 1955), 434.

1854   L'Express (Paris), 20 July 1956, p. 16.

1855   *Information*, 69 (October 1955), 53.

1856   *Jubilee*, 3 (August 1955), 51.

1857   *Kirkus*, 23 (1 May 1955), 308.

1858   *New Yorker*, 31 (9 July 1955), 83.

OFFICERS AND GENTLEMEN con't.

1859 *Time*, 66 (11 July 1955), 98.

1860 *Times Literary Supplement*, 8 July 1955, p. 377.

1861 *Today*, 11 (December 1955), 30.

1862 *Wisconsin Library Bulletin*, 51 (September 1955), 12.

THE ORDEAL OF GILBERT PINFOLD

1863 Bory, Jean-Louis. "Lorsque le diable pince sans rire: l'épreuve de Gilbert Pinfold," *L'Express* (Paris), 10 February 1959, pp. 28-29.

1864 Doyle, Paul A., and Alan Clodd. "A British *Pinfold* and an American *Pinfold*," *Evelyn Waugh Newsletter*, 3, iii (Winter 1969), 1-5.

1865 Elsen, Claude. Preface to the French translation of *The Ordeal of Gilbert Pinfold*. Paris: Stock, 1957.

Reviews

1866 Alpert, Hollis. *Saturday Review*, 40 (17 August 1957), 15.

1867 Bullock, F. T. *New York Herald Tribune Book Review*, 11 August 1957, p. 4.

1868 Burke, O. *Jubilee*, 5 (September 1957), 44.

1869 Cosman, Max. *Carolina Quarterly*, 10, No. 1 (Fall 1957), 69-72.

1870 Engle, Paul. *Chicago Sunday Tribune*, 11 August 1957, p. 3.

1871   Gilpatrick, N. *Extension,* 52 (October 1957), 39.

1872   Hogan, William. *San Francisco Chronicle,* 12 August
         1957, p. 21.

1873   Hughes, Riley. *Catholic World,* 185 (September 1957),
         471.

1874   Lalou, Rene. *La Nouvelles Littéraires,* 20 November
         1958.

1875   Maddocks, Melvin. *Christian Science Monitor,* 15 August
         1957, p. 7.

1876   McEwen, R. *Month,* 18 NS (October 1957), 247.

1877   McLaughlin, Richard. *Springfield Republican,* 29 Sep-
         tember 1957, p. 8.

1878   O'Donnell, Donat. *Spectator,* 19 July 1957, p. 112.

1879   Price, Martin. *Yale Review,* 47 (Autumn 1957), 150.

1880   Raymond, John. *New Statesman,* 54 (20 July 1957), 88.

1881   Rolo, Charles. *Atlantic,* 200 (November 1957), 244.

1882   Sarton, May. *Nation,* 185 (31 August 1957), 96.

1883   Shrapnel, Norman. *Manchester Guardian,* 23 July 1957,
         p. 4.

1884   Stopp, F. J. *Renascence,* 10 (Winter 1957), 94-99.

1885   Sykes, Gerald. *New York Times,* 11 August 1957, p. 4.

1886   Walbridge, E. F. *Library Journal,* 82 (July 1957), 1781.

1887   *Ave Maria,* 86 (17 August 1957), 23.

1888   *Best Sellers,* 17 (15 August 1957), 156.

THE ORDEAL OF GILBERT PINFOLD reviews con't.

1899 *Booklist,* 54 (1 September 1957), 22.

1890 *Critic,* 16 (September 1957), 35.

1891 *Kirkus,* 25 (1 June 1957), 396.

1892 *New Yorker,* 33 (17 August 1957), 107.

1893 *Sign,* 37 (October 1957), 70.

1894 *Tablet,* 210 (20 July 1957), 60.

1895 *Time,* 70 (12 August 1957), 92.

1896 *Time,* (Atlantic edition), 70, No. 7 (1957), 58.

1897 *Times Literary Supplement,* 19 July 1957, 437.

THE WORLD OF EVELYN WAUGH

1898 Engle, Paul. *Chicago Sunday Tribune,* 27 April 1958,
      p. 4.

1899 Hill, W. *Best Sellers,* 18 (15 May 1958), 76.

1900 Hogan, William. *San Francisco Chronicle,* 11 April
      1958, p. 27.

1901 Oboler, E. M. *Library Journal,* 83 (1 April 1958), 1086.

1902 Sykes, Gerald. *New York Times,* 13 April 1958, p. 5.

1903 *New York Herald Tribune Book Review,* 25 May 1958,
      p. 13.

1904   *Time*, 71 (21 April 1958), p. 94.

MGR. RONALD KNOX

1905   Gwynn, D. "Evelyn Waugh and Ronald Knox," *Irish Ecclesiastical Record*, 105 (May 1966), 288-301.

1906   Wheeler, Gordon. "Waugh on Knox: An Appraisal," *Dublin Review*, 233 (1959), 346-352.

Reviews

1907   Barton, John M. T. *Month*, 22 NS (December 1959), 365-367.

1908   Betjeman, John. *New Yorker*, 36 (23 April 1960), 174.

1909   Brady, Charles A. *New York Times Book Review*, 24 January 1960, p. 6.

1910   Cartwright, John. *Catholic Historical Review*, 46, No. 4 (January 1961), 465.

1911   Clancy, Joseph. *America*, 13 February 1960, p. 589.

1912   Clancy, William. *Commonweal*, 72 (1 April 1960), 19.

1913   Connolly, P. *Furrow*, 10 (November 1959), 737.

1914   Dwyer, J. J. *Clergy Review*, 45 (February 1960), 98-104.

1915   Forrest, M. *Homiletic and Pastoral Review*, 45 (February 1960), 483.

1916   Gannon, Robert I. *New York Herald Tribune Book Review*, 21 February 1960, p. 3.

MGR. RONALD KNOX reviews con't.

1917   Gleason, J. B. *San Francisco Chronicle*, 14 February 1960, p. 17.

1918   Higgins, George G. *Commonweal* (26 February 1960), 600.

1919   Hill, W. *Best Sellers*, 19 (1 February 1960), 370.

1920   Hollis, C. *Critic*, 18 (March 1960), 32.

1921   Houlihan, Thomas F. *Library Journal*, 85 (1 January 1960), 110.

1922   Johnson, Paul. *New Statesman*, 58 (10 October 1959), 482.

1923   La Farge, John. *Saturday Review*, 43 (5 March 1960), 25.

1924   Leslie, Shane. *National Review* (13 February 1960), 110.

1925   Mathew, G. *Blackfriars*, 41 (February 1960), 37.

1926   McLaughlin, Richard. *Springfield Republican*, 14 February 1960, p. 56.

1927   Murray, S. W. *Evangelical Quarterly*, 32 (October-December 1960), 242-243.

1928   O'Brian, John. *Chicago Sunday Tribune*, 21 February 1960, p. 2.

1929   O'Donovan, Patrick. *New Republic*, 142 (4 April 1960), 25.

1930   Pickrel, Paul. *Harper's* (March 1960), 114.

1931   Poore, Charles. *New York Times*, 3 March 1960, p. 27.

1932   Rope, H. *Pax*, 50 (September 1960), 25-27.

1933   Sheed, W. *Jubilee*, 7 (February 1960), 49.

1934   Shepherd, L. *Critic*, 18 (May 1960), 58 *passim*.

1935   Snape, H. C. *Modern Churchman*, NS 3 (June 1960), 174-176.

1936   Spark, Muriel. *Twentieth Century* (January 1960), 83.

1937   Stella, Maris. *Commonweal*, 71 (26 February 1960), 601.

1938   Sykes, Christopher. *Spectator* (9 October 1959), 484.

1939   Wilson, Angus. *Encounter* (January 1960), 78.

1940   *Booklist*, 56 (2 March 1960), 415.

1941   *Catholic Charities Review*, 46 (December 1962), 20.

1942   *Catholic Educator*, 30 (March 1960), 538.

1943   *Christian Century*, 77 (3 February 1960), 139.

1944   *Information*, 74 (April 1960), 56.

1945   *Kirkus*, 27 (15 November 1959), 860.

1946   *Priest*, 16 (June 1960), 568.

1947   *Sign*, 39 (April 1960), 62.

1948   *Studies*, 49 (September 1960), 84.

1949   *Tablet*, 213 (10 October 1959), 857.

1950   *Tablet*, 214 (2 April 1960), 328-329.

1951   *Times Literary Supplement*, 9 October 1959, p. 569.

TOURIST IN AFRICA

1952   Allot, Anthony. *Tablet,* 24 September 1960, p. 870.

1953   Carter, Gwendolyn M. *New York Herald Tribune Lively Arts,* 19 February 1961, p. 27.

1954   Corke, Hilary. *Listener,* 29 September 1960, p. 524.

1955   Cosman, Max. *Commonweal,* 73 (6 January 1961), 392.

1956   Davidson, Basil. *New Statesman,* 60 (24 September 1960), 439.

1957   Hogan, William. *San Francisco Chronicle,* 14 November 1960, p. 39.

1958   Hughes, John. *Christian Science Monitor,* 17 November 1960, p. 15.

1959   Hutchens, J. K. *New York Herald Tribune Book Review,* 8 November 1960, p. 23.

1960   Huxley, Elspeth. *New York Times Book Review,* 20 November 1960, p. 3.

1961   Igoe, W. J. *Chicago Sunday Tribune,* 13 November 1960, p. 3.

1962   Jackson, Katherine G. *Harper's,* 22 (February 1961), 106.

1963   Jacobson, Dan. *Spectator,* 23 September 1960, p. 448.

1964   Mathew, G. *Blackfriars,* 41 (November 1960), 443.

1965   Maxwell, Gavin. *Manchester Guardian,* 7 October 1960, p. 15.

1966   McNaspy, C. J. *America,* 104 (7 January 1961), 451.

1967   Poore, Charles. *New York Times*, 8 November 1960,
      p. 27.

1968   Ready, W. *Critic*, 19 (January 1961), 32.

1969   Sherry, John. *Book of the Month Club News*, November
      1960, p. 9.

1970   Sillitoe, Alan. *Time and Tide*, 15 October 1960, 1226.

1971   Smith, William J. *English Journal*, 50 (February 1961),
      p. 142.

1972   --- *New Republic*, 144 (23 January 1961), 19.

1973   Wills, G. *National Review*, 19 November 1960, p. 327.

1974   Young, B. A. *Punch*, 12 October 1960, p. 539.

1975   *Ave Maria*, 93 (24 January 1961), 24.

1976   *Booklist*, 57 (15 November 1960), 175.

1977   *Bookmark*, 20 (December 1960), 651.

1978   *English Journal*, 50 (February 1961), 142.

1979   *Newsweek*, 14 November 1960, 114.

1980   *New Yorker*, 36 (26 November 1960), 238.

1981   *Time*, 76 (28 November 1960), 100.

1982   *Wisconsin Library Bulletin*, 57 (May 1961), 180.

1983   *Times Literary Supplement*, 23 September 1960, 603.

UNCONDITIONAL SURRENDER
(The End of the Battle)

1984   Amis, Kingsley. *Spectator*, 207 (27 October 1961), 581-
       582.

1985   Bergonzi, Bernard. *Manchester Guardian*, 27 October
       1961, p. 7.

1986   Boatwright, Taliaferro. *New York Herald Tribune Books*,
       7 January 1962, p. 5.

1987   E. C. *Books Abroad*, Spring, 1962, p. 207.

1988   Cevasco, G. *Sign*, 41 (March 1962), 70.

1989   Coffey, W. *Ramparts*, 1 (May 1962), 94.

1990   Derrick, Christopher. *Tablet*, 215 (28 October 1961),
       1024, 1026.

1991   Didion, Joan. *National Review*, 12 (27 March 1962), 215.

1992   Fuller, John. *Listener*, 26 October 1961, p. 665.

1993   Gardiner, Harold. *America*, 106 (27 January 1962), 564.

1994   Heller, Josph. *Nation*, 194 (20 January 1962), 62.

1995   Highet, Gilbert. *Book of the Month Club News*, January
       1962, p. 7.

1996   Hynes, Sam. *Commonweal*, 75 (2 February 1962), 495.

1997   Jacobson, Dan. *New Leader*, 45 (14 May 1962), 10.

1998   Kermode, Frank. *Partisan Review*, 2 (Summer 1962), 466.

1999   Lowrey, Burling. *Saturday Review*, 45 (6 January 1962),
       65.

2000 Maddocks, Melvin. *Christian Science Monitor*, 11 January 1962, p. 7.

2001 McDonnell, T. P. *Catholic World*, 194 (March 1962), 365.

2002 O'Donovan, Patrick. *New Republic*, 146 (12 February 1962), 21.

2003 Pickrel, Paul. *Harper's*, 224 (February 1962), 106.

2004 Prescott, Orville. *New York Times*, 8 January 1962, p. 37.

2005 --- *San Francisco Chronicle*, 16 January 1962, p. 33.

2006 Price, R. G. G. *Punch*, 1 November 1961, p. 659.

2007 Pritchett, V. S. *New Statesman*, 62 (26 October 1961), 603.

2008 Quinton, Anthony. *Time and Tide*, 26 October 1961, p. 1801.

2009 Raven, Simon. *London Magazine*, November 1961, p. 72.

2010 Ready, W. *Critic*, 20 (March 1962), 70.

2011 Ryan S. *Ave Maria*, 95 (10 March 1962), 28.

2012 Sale, Roger. *Hudson Review*, Spring, 1962, p. 134.

2013 Sullivan, Richard. *Chicago Sunday Tribune Magazine of Books*, 7 January 1962, p. 1.

2014 Toynbee, Philip. *Observer*, 29 October 1961, p. 21.

2015 Traynor, John. *Extension*, 56 (April 1962), 36.

2016 Vidal, Gore. *New York Times Book Review*, 7 January 1962, p. 1. Reprinted in *Rocking the Boat*. Boston: Little, Brown, 1962. Pp. 235-243.

UNCONDITIONAL SURRENDER con't.

2017   Weeks, Edward. *Atlantic*, 209 (February 1962), 114.

2018   Wood, Frederick. *English Studies*, 43 (June 1962), 209.

2019   *Best Sellers*, 21 (15 January 1962), 410.

2020   *Booklist*, 58 (15 February 1962), 371.

2021   *Extension*, 56 (April 1962), 36.

2022   *Jubilee*, 9 (March 1962), 47.

2023   *Kirkus*, 29 (15 September 1961), 853.

2024   *London Times Weekly Review*, 2 November 1961, p. 10.

2025   *Month*, NS 27 (March 1962), 186.

2026   *Newsweek*, 59 (15 January 1962), 82.

2027   *Time*, 79 (19 January 1962), 84.

2028   *Times Literary Supplement*, 27 October 1961, p. 770.

BASIL SEAL RIDES AGAIN

2029   Brooke, Jocelyn. *Listener*, 70 (7 November 1963), 764.

2030   Carew, Rivers. *Dubliner*, 3 (Spring 1964), 72-73.

2031   Jones, Dan. *New York Review of Books*, 20 February 1964, p. 3.

2032   Pritchett, V. S. *New Statesman*, 66 (15 November 1963), 706.

2033   Pryce-Jones, Alan. *New York Herald Tribune*, 11 December 1963, p. 27.

2034   *London Times Weekly Review*, 7 November 1963, p. 11.

2035   *Punch*, 245 (13 November 1963), 725.

2036   *Times Literary Supplement*, 14 November 1963, p. 921.

A LITTLE LEARNING

2037   Auden, W. H. *New Yorker*, 41 (3 April 1965), 159.

2038   Barrett, William. *Atlantic*, 215 (January 1965), 127.

2039   Bedford, S. *New York Herald Tribune Book Week*, 15 November 1964, p. 3.

2040   Berolzheimer, H. F. *Library Journal*, 90 (15 January 1965), 240.

2041   Bradbury, Malcolm. *Spectator*, 11 September 1964, p. 347.

2042   Burgess, Anthony. *Encounter*, 23 (December 1964), 64.

2043   Caird, J. B. *Library Review*, Winter 1964, p. 359.

2044   Daiches, David. *New York Times*, 1 November 1964, p. 4.

2045   Davis, R. M. *Modern Language Journal*, 49 (November 1965), 458.

2046   Day, Dorothy. *Critic*, 23 (February-March 1965), 74.

2047   Doyle, P. A. *Best Sellers*, 24 (15 November 1964), 322.

A LITTLE LEARNING con't.

2048   Eimerl, Sarel. *Reporter*, 31 (3 December 1964), 55.

2049   Fadiman, C. *Book of the Month Club News*, December 1964, p. 10.

2050   Flaherty, D. L. *America*, 111 (10 October 1964), 415.

2051   Gersh, Gabriel. *South Atlantic Quarterly*, 64 (Summer 1965), 425.

2052   Gloag, Julian. *Saturday Review*, 47 (14 November 1964), 36.

2053   Gross, John. *New York Review of Books*, 3 (13 December 1964), 4.

2054   Hart, Jeffrey. *National Review*, 16 (29 December 1964), 1152.

2055   Heyne, P. T. *Cresset*, 28 (January 1965), 24.

2056   Igoe, W. J. *Chicago Sunday Tribune*, 13 December 1964, p. 10.

2057   Kauffmann, Stanley. *New Republic*, 151 (21 November 1964), 23.

2058   Lambert, G. W. *Bookman* (London), September 1964, pp. 9-11.

2059   Las Vergnas, Raymond. *Les Nouvelles Littéraires*, 27 June 1968.

2060   Marsh, Pamela. *Christian Science Monitor*, 5 November 1964, p. 116.

2061   Moore, Brian. *Harper's*, 229 (December 1964), 130.

2062   Muggeridge, Malcolm. *Esquire*, 63 (February 1965), 56.

2063 Murray, James G. *America*, 111 (12 December 1964), 782.

2064 Plomer, William. *Listener*, 72 (10 September 1964), 397.

2065 Powers, J. F. *Commonweal*, 81 (4 December 1964), 359.

2066 Prescott, Orville. *New York Times*, 4 November 1964, p. 37.

2067 Pritchett, V. S. *New Statesman*, 68 (25 September 1964), 445.

2068 Pryce-Jones, Alan. *New York Herald Tribune*, 3 November 1964, p. 19.

2069 --- *Commonweal*, 81 (4 December 1964), 343.

2070 Shanahan, W. J. *Catholic World*, 65 (February 1965), 315.

2071 Stratford, P. *Saturday Night*, 80 (April 1965), 28.

2072 Waugh, Alec. *Cosmopolitan*, November 1964, p. 26.

2073 Weintraub, S. *Books Abroad*, 39 (Summer 1965), 354.

2074 Wolff, J. *Today*, 20 (February 1965), 30.

2075 Woodruff, Douglas. *Tablet*, 218 (12 September 1964), 1029.

2076 *Choice*, 2 (March 1965), 24.

2077 *Economist*, 212 (12 September 1964), 1031.

2078 *Month*, 32 (December 1964), 339.

2079 *National Observer*, 5 (18 April 1966), 21.

2080 *Newsweek*, 14 (9 November 1964), 104.

2081 *Playboy*, 12 (January 1965), 38.

A LITTLE LEARNING con't.

2082   *Time*, 84 (13 November 1964), 134.

2083   *Times Literary Supplement*, 10 September 1964, p. 836.

SWORD OF HONOUR

2084   Bogaards, Winnifred M. "The Conclusion of Waugh's Trilogy: Three Variants," *Evelyn Waugh Newsletter*, 4 (Autumn 1970), 6-7.

2085   Braybrooke, Neville. "Evelyn Waugh en uniforme," *La Vie Intellectuelle*, 27 (April 1956), 135-140.

2086   Burrows, L. R. "Scenes de la Vie Militaire," *Westerly* (1962), No. 1, 3-6.

2087   Costello, Patrick. "An Idea of Comedy and Waugh's Sword of Honour," *Kansas Quarterly*, 1 (Summer 1969), 41-50.

2088   Davis, Robert Murray. "Guy Crouchback's Children--A Reply," *English Language Notes*, 7 (1969/70), 127-129. Reply to Mattingly, "Guy Crouchback's 'Children.' "

2089   Delbaere-Garant, J. " 'Who shall inherit England?' A Comparison between *Howards End*, *Parade's End* and *Unconditional Surrender*," *English Studies*, 50 (1969), 101-105.

2090   Engelborghs, Maurits. "Het laatste werk van Evelyn Waugh (*Officers and Gentlemen*)," *Dietsche Warande en Belfort*, (Antwerp) 3 (1956), 167-177.

2091 Hart, Jeffrey. "The Roots of Honor," *National Review*, 18 (1966), 168-169.

2092 Kiely, Robert. "The Craft of Despondency--The Traditional Novelists," *Daedalus*, 92 (1963), 220-237.

2093 Mattingly, Joseph F. "Guy Crouchback's 'Children,' " *English Language Notes*, 6 (1968/69), 200-201. See reply by Davis, "Guy Crouchback's Children."

2094 Phillips, Gene D. "Waugh's *Sword of Honour* on BBC-TV," *Evelyn Waugh Newsletter*, 4, iii (Winter 1970), 3-4.

2095 Rutherford, Andrew. "Waugh's Sword of Honour," in Maynard Mack and Ian Gregor (eds.), *Imagined Worlds: Essays on some English Novels and Novelists in Honour of John Butt*. London: Methuen, 1968. Pp. 441-460.

2096 St. John, John. "Temporary Officers and Gentlemen," *Sunday Times*, 7 September 1969, p. 10.

2097 Semple, H. E. "Evelyn Waugh's Modern Crusade," *English Studies in Africa*, 11 (1968), 47-59.

2098 Stopp, Frederick J. "Waugh: End of An Illusion," *Renascence*, 9 (1956/57), 59-67, 76.

2099 Voorhees, Richard J. "Evelyn Waugh's War Novels," *Queen's Quarterly*, 65 (1958/59), 53-63.

Reviews

2100 Murphy, M. *Downside Review*, 84 (January 1966), 112.

2101 Raven, S. *Spectator*, 12 June 1964, p. 798.

2102 Restaino, K. M. *Catholic World*, 205 (August 1967), 314.

2103 Sullivan, R. *Books Today*, 3 (11 December 1966), 10.

SWORD OF HONOUR reviews con't.

2104 *Choice*, 4 (June 1967), 424.

2105 *Kirkus*, 34 (15 September 1966), 1009.

2106 *Prairie Schooner*, 42 (Fall 1968), 279.

2107 *Times Literary Supplement*, 17 March 1966, p. 216.

INDEX

A. A. 1423

A., M. 1482

Abraham, Dr. Johnston 422

Abrahams, William 1585

Ackerley, J. R. 390

Acton, Harold 172, 178, 842, 843.

Agate, James 1424, 1465

Aiken, Conrad 1313

Albérès, R. M. 844

Aldington, Richard 1367

Alexander, Calvert 845

Allen, G. W. 817

Allen, W. G. 1745

Allen, W. Gore 846

Allen, Walter 847

Allot, Anthony 1952

Allott, Kenneth 427

Allsop, Kenneth 664a, 847a, 1292

Alpert, Hollis 1866

Amis, Kingsley 1010, 1111, 1829, 1984

Angeli, Helen Rossetti 478, 498

Anson, Peter 529

Argus, Jan 1147

Arlen, Michael 421, 1314

Armitage, Gilbert 1442

Arnau, Frank 538

Aslin, Elizabeth 547

Athill, Laurence I. 1532

Attwater, Donald 1533

Auden, W. H. 419, 459, 583, 2037

Austin, Alfred 506

Avedon, Richard 526

B., F. 1407

B., H. P. 1466

Bachelor Abroad, A see *Labels*

Backhouse, Gerald 229

Baker, Denys Val 1103

Balfour, Patrick ["Mr. Gossip," Lord Kinross], 400, 431, 789, 826, 848-856

Bannington, T. J. 857, 1139

Barnett, William F. 858

Barr, Donald 1812

Barrett, William 2038

Barry, Iris 1523, 1715

Barton, John M. T. 1907

Barton, Margaret 412

Basil Seal Rides Again 35, 152, 2029-2036

Bates, H. E. 430

Bawden, Edward 384

Bayes, Walter 395

Bayley, John 1129, 1703

Beachcroft, T. O. 431

Beary, Thomas John 859, 1606

Beaton, Cecil 542, 860

Beattie, A. M. 861

Bedford, Sybille 511, 2039

Bedoyere, Count Michael de la 1534

Beeger, Susanne 1607

Beer, Otto F. 865

Beerbohm, Max 96, 352, 552

Bell, E. T. 418

"Bella Fleace Gave a Party" 13, 24, 29, 73, 119, 141, 149

Belloc, Hilaire 52, 454, 499, 505, 616, 623

Belvedere, J. 1746, 1769

Benedict, Stewart H. 866

Bender, Elaine 1337

Bengar, F. 385

Bennett, Arnold 1342, 1368

Benson, Robert Hugh 47, 351

Benson, Theodora 66, 453

Benstock, Bernard 817, 866a

Bentley, Nicolas 118, 120, 866b

Beresford, J. D. 1629

Bergengruen, Werner 1073

Bergonzi, Bernard 867-869, 1467, 1985

Bernanos, Georges 430

Berolzheimer, H. F. 2040

Berry, Ana M. 387

Betjeman, John 434, 491, 500, 870-871, 1234, 1908

Birkenhead, Lord 872-873

Black Mischief 8, 13, 116, 774, 1142, 1237, 1422-1441

Black, Stephen 658- 659

Blumenberg, Hans 874

Boatwright, Taliaferro 1986

Bodelsen, C. A. 551, 875

Bogaards, Winnifred M. 796, 803, 827, 2084

Bono, Marshal de 411

Borchner, George 393

Borrello, Alfred 876-877

Bory, Jean-Louis 1863

Bowen, Elizabeth 482

Bower, Anthony 1586

Bowra, C. M. 878, 1524

Boyle, Alexander 879

Boyle, R. 880

Boyle, Stuart 39

Boyle, Vera 39

Bradbury, Malcolm 816, 1545, 2041

Bradford, Curtis 1830

Bradley, H. Dennis 790

Brady, Charles A. 84, 881-882, 1909

Brande, Dorothea 1425

Brander, Donald M. 883

Braybrooke, Neville 821, 884-885, 2085

Bregy, Katherine 1716

Breit, Harvey 886-887

Brennan, Neil Francis 828

Brideshead Revisited 14, 74, 136, 367, 682, 888, 1606-1666

Bridie, James 462

Brien, Alan 889

Brighouse, Harold 1682

Broderick, John 1683

Brome, Vincent 521

Brooke, Jocelyn 2029

Brophy, Brigid 890, 1468, 1546

Bruce, C. G. 400

Brumini, John G. 73

Buckley, William F. 892

Bullock, F. T. 1867

Burbridge, Rober T. 1459

Burdett, Francis 1547

Burgess, Anthony 893-896, 2042

Burke, O. 1868

Burnett, Hugh 663

Burnham, Philip 1483

Burr, Jane 759

Burra, Peter J. S. 1318

Burrows, L. R. 2086

Bush, G. 1548

Butcher, Maryvonne 897

"By Special Request" 13

Byron, Robert 413, 1246

C., E. 1987

C., T. 1443

Caird, J. B. 2043

Calder, Angus 898

Calder-Marshall, Arthur 423-424

Cameron, J. M. 657, 899-901

Campbell, Roy 1185, 1319

Campion, Edmund 94, 574

Cantwell, Robert 1426

Capote, Truman 526

Caraman, Philip 46, 534, 902

Carens, James F. 817, 819, 821, 829, 903

Carew, Dudley 762, 904

Carew, Rivers 2030

Carroll, Lewis 463

Carson, Anthony 55, 532

Cartensen, Broder 905

Carter, Gwendolyn M. 1953

Cartwright, John 1910

Casey, George 906

Cassen, Bernard 907

Caven, Stewart 718

Cayton, R. F. 817

Cecchin, Giovanni 908

Cecil, Lord David 552

Cerf, Bennett 73, 1587

Cevasco, G. 1988

Chaigne, Louis 1522

Chamberlain, C. L. 909-910, 1588

Chamberlain, Peter 416

Channon, Sir Henry 911

Chapin, John 89, 92

Chaplin, Charlie 335

Chapman, Guy 417

Chapman, Ronald 536

Charques, R. D. 1747

Chastaing, Maxine 912-913

Chauveau, Paul 1427, 1469

Chesterman, Hugh 62

Chesterton, G. K. 537, 683, 934

Childers, James S. 389

Chilton, E. E. 1630

Chimay, Jacqueline de 60

Christiansen, Arthur 914

Christina of Markyate 527

Churchill, Randolph 516, 915

Churchill, Thomas 830a, 1608

Clancy, Joseph 1911

Clancy, William 1912

Cleveland, June 453

Clicquot-Pousardin, Mme. Veuve 60

Clinton, Farley 916-917

Clinton-Baddeley, V. C. 1631

Clodd, Alan 1609, 1864

Clonmore, Lord 435 (See Earl of Wicklow)

Clynes, Rt. Hon. J. R. 438

Cochran, Charles B. 464

Coffey, W. 1989

Cogley, John 647, 918, 1610

Cohen, Martin S. 1460, 1611

Cohen, Nathan 919

Coleman, John 1662

Collingridge, A. C. 920

Collins, G. E. P. 426

Colmer, John 1060

Compton-Burnett, Ivy 519, 524

Connolly, Cyril 455, 581, 585, 826, 922-925a, 1253, 1343, 1704 (See Palinurus)

Connolly, Francis X. 73, 1667, 1770

Connolly, P. 1913

Constantine, Mrrray 414

Constantius 324

Conway, Pierre 926

Cook, Luella B. 791

Cook, William J., Jr. 818, 830

Cooke, Alistair 1717

Cooper, Diana 927-928

Cooper, Lettice 450

Cooperman, Stanley 1831

Corke, Hilary 1954

Corbishley, T. 825

Corr, Patricia 929-930

Cosman, Max 931, 1808, 1869, 1955

Costello, Patrick 2087

Cotter, J. 1832

Cousins, Norman 1684

Cowley, Malcolm 1408, 1428

Coxe, Howard 1369

Coxe, L. O. 1813, 1833

Craft, Robert 932

Craven, T. 1320

Crease, Francis 38

Croft, Noel A. C. 439

Cronin, Anthony 933

Crowell, Norton B. 506

Crozier, Mary 662

"Cruise" 13, 24, 29, 75, 120

Cruttwell, C.R.M.F. 1056, 1270

Cunard, Emerald 985

Cunard, Nancy 985

Cuneo, P. 1834

Cunningham-Grahame, R. B. 437

"The Curse of the Race" 29, 64

Daiches, David 2044

Daly, Maureen 73

Dangerfield, George 1589

D'Arcy, Martin C., S. J. 858, 935

Dauch, Alfred 832

D'Avanzo, Mario L. 1614

Davenport, John 847a, 1292, 1370, 1718

Davidson, Angus 446

Davidson, Basil 1956

Davies, Jack 659

Davin, Daniel J. 82

Davis, Robert Murray 78, 797, 803, 816, 817, 819, 823, 826, 831, 936-942, 1366, 1461, 1544, 1612-1613, 2045, 2088

Dawson 1185

Day, Dorothy 2046

Dayrelle, Vivienne (Mrs. Graham Greene) 63

Decline and Fall 4, 76, 768, 776, 792b, 1101, 1129a, 1337-1362

Decline and Fall (film) 1340

Dedijer, Vladimer 492

Dedmon, Emmett 1685, 1719

Delasanta, Rodney 1614

Delbaere-Garant, J. 2089

Dennis, Nigel 943

Derrick, Christopher 1990

Deschner, Karlheinz 944

Desta, Ras 293

Dever, Joe 945, 1740

DeVitis, A. A. 820, 833

Devlin, Christopher 514

Dickens, Charles 496

Didion, Joan 1991

Dollen, Charles 948

"Domino" 949

Donaldson, Francis 821

Dooley, D. J. 834, 950-
952

Dos Passos, John 397

Douglas, Norman 383

Downey, K. 70a

Doyle, Paul A. 798-803, 822,
953-959, 1338, 1615-1616,
1864, 2047

"Dragoman" 768

Drescher, Horst W. 1192

Driberg, Tom [Dragoman]
573, 675-676, 960-965

Drinkwater, John 416

Duer, Harriet Whitney 835

Duggan, Alfred 58, 377, 507

Duguid, Julian 395

Du Mont, C. A. Neven 217

Dunlop, R. O. 591

Dunsany, Lord 449

Durand, Mortimer 408

Dutton, Ralph 503

Dwyer, J. J. 1914

Dyson, A. F. 956, 966-967

Eagleton, Terry 968

Edmund Campion 12, 92, 326,
1481-1522

Edschmid, Kasimir 393

Edstrom, David 449

Edwards, John D. 969

Eichelbaum, S. 1705

Eimerl, Sarel 970, 2048

Ellis, A. E. 1470

Ellis, G. U. 971

Elmen, Paul 825

Elsen, Claude 1865

Elton, Lord 449

Engelborghs, Maurits 2090

Engle, Paul 825, 1870, 1898

English, William A. 804

"Englishman's Home, An" 24,
29

Ervine, St. John 1371

Etzkorn, L. R. 1501

Evans, Ernestine 1686

Evans, Joan 502

"Excursion in Reality" 13, 24,
29, 117, 118

Faber, Father 536

Fadiman, Clifton 1549, 2049

Farago, Ladislas 486

Farr, D. Paul 805, 977-978

Faulkner, William 980-981

Fausset, H. 1748

Featherstone, Joseph 982

Fedden, Henry R. 442

Fellini, Frederico 358

Ferguson, Otis 1550

Fermor, Patrick Leigh 493

Fernald 1315

Ferri, Paula 983

Fielding, Daphne 56, 540,
984-985

Fielding, Gabriel 986-987

Firbank, Ronald 191, 1254

Firebrace, Ethel 432

FISH 226

Fitts, Dudley 1372

Fitzgerald, D. 1771, 1835

FitzGerald, Gregory 75

Flaherty, D. L. 2050

"Flat in London, A" (Serial
of *A Handful of Dust*) 125,
126, 1390

Fleming, [Robert] Peter 396,
405, 422, 675, 988, 1344,
1409, 1444, 1668

Flood, E. 989

Forbes-Boyd, Eric 1669

Ford, Anne 685

Ford, Boris 1110

Ford, F. E. 1151

Ford, J. N. C. 1151

Forrest, M. 1915

Foxwell, Ivan 792b

Frank, Joseph 1772

Frank, Waldo 393

Franklin, M.A.E. 1310

Fraser, G. S. 990

Freeman, John 661-663

Fremantle, Anne 991-992, 1502,
1632, 1802

Fricker, Robert 993

Friedman, Melvin J. 1266

Friedmann 944

Froshaug, E. P. C. 1535

Fuerst, W. R. 385

Fulford, R. T. B. 777, 825

Fuller, John 1992

Fulton, Mary 748

Fulton, Francis 994

G., A. E. M. 1429

G., J. M. S. 1345

Gadd, Thomas W. 995

Gallagher, D. S. 806-807

Galsworthy, John 57

Gannon, Robert I. 1916

Gardiner, Harold 682, 996-997,
1159, 1633, 1749, 1814,
1836, 1993

Gardner, Erle Stanley 877

Gardner, Evelyn. See Evelyn
Gardner Waugh

Gardner, Mona 461

Garnett, David 1536

Garrison, W. E. 1634

Gaul, C. C. 1750

Gawin, John 826

Gay, R. M. 1590

Gehman, Richard 80

Gerhardie, William 1001a
[formerly Gerhardi]

Gernsheim, Helmut 508

Gersh, Gabriel 2051

Gervais, Albert 398

Gibbings, Robert 395

Gibbs, Wolcott 1720

Gilpatrick, N. 1871

Gingrich, Arnold 100

Giradoux, Jean 1422

Glanz, Luzia 1002

Gleason, J. B. 1917

Gleason, James 1003

Glen, Alexander R. 439,
1004

Gloag, Julian 2052

Gloucester, Duke of 204,
206

Goldman, Penryn 395

Goldring, Douglas 1005-
1006

Goolden, Barbara 766

Gorden, Jan and Cora 392

Gordon, Caroline 1008

"Gossip, Mr." 669

Götz, Karl-August 1007

Gould, Francis Carruthers 387

Gould, Gerald 1346, 1373, 1430

Gower, William 1570

Grace, William J. 1009

Graham, W. S. 1721

Graves, Robert 467

Gray, James 1773, 1837

Green, Martin 1010

Green, Peter 1462

Greenblatt, Stephen Jay 823

Greene, Graham 95-96, 458,
466, 474, 475, 487, 488, 509,
545, 589, 600, 618a, 683, 934,
1012-1013, 1073, 1108-1111,
1202, 1241, 1484

Greenidge, John 778

Greenidge, Terrence 388, 429,
1014-1017, 1269, 1316-1317

Gregor, Jan 2007

Grenville, Sir Richard 414

Gribble, Thomas 1018

Griffiths, Joan 1019

Grimley, Fr. Bernard 1020

Gross, John 2053

"Grosvenor, John" 1021

Gruhl, Max 389

Guenther, John 1022a

Guthrie, Eric 83

Gutteridge, Bernard 1023

Gwynn, D. 1905

H., C. B. 1024

H., W. H. 1687

Hackney, Alan 792b

Hadfield, John 82

Hall, James 1025-1026

Hamerton, F. M. 1151

Hamilton, Cicely 444

Hamnett, Nina 1027

Hanbury-Tracy, John 453

Handford, Basil W. T. 1028

Handful of Dust, A 11, 77, 573, 1050, 1107, 1459-1480. See also "By Special Request," "A Flat in London," and "The Man Who Liked Dickens"

Hanley, James 450

Hansen-Löve, Friedrich 1029

Hansford-Johnson, Pamela 427

Hardy, John Edward 1617

Hardy, Thomas 194

Harrington, Edmund 1030

Harris, Frank 521

Harris, M. G. 1031

Hart, Jeffrey 1032-1033, 1966, 2091

Hart-Davis, Rupert 552

Hartley, L. P. 1374

Harty, E. R. 1618

Hass, V. P. 1838

Hassell, W. O. 501

Hatfield, John 93

Hawton, Hector 1137

Haynes, E. S. P. 1035

Heilman, Robert B. 1619

Helena 25, 145, 791a, 1740-1767

Helena, Saint 101, 102, 338, 340, 347, 349a, 606-607

Heller, Joseph 1994

Hemingway, Ernest 429, 483, 484, 980-981, 1161

Henderson, R. W. 1751

Hennessy, C. P. 1036

Hennessey, Joseph 1234

Henslowe, Leonard 65

Herbert, Mary 1022

Herr, Dan 88

Heyne, P. T. 2055

Hickey, William, See Tom Drieberg

Higgins, George C. 1918

Higginson, Teresa 579

Highet, Gilbert 1995

Hill, W. 1899, 1919

Hillier, Bevis 1037

Hills, L. Rust 100

Hilton, James 1774

Hinchcliffe, Peter 1038

Hines, Leo 1039

Hitchcock, Alfred 80

Hitler, Adolph 593

Hoare, Rawdon 398

Hobhouse, Chris. B. 1393

Hodge, Alan 467

Hoehn, Matthew 1040

Hogan, William 1872, 1900, 1957

Hogarth, William 504

Hohoff, Curt 1041

Holliday, Terence 1471, 1551

Hollis, Christopher 554, 824, 1042-1043, 1185, 1339, 1809, 1920

Holman-Hunt, Diana 97, 533, 1044

Holman-Hunt, William 533

Holmstrom, Dorothy 791

Holt, Edgar 1394

Holy Places, The 27, 1802-1807

Hooper, Minor 717

Horchler, R. T. 1839

Horder, J. P. 1525

Horgan, Paul 1395

Horne, Roger 1047

Hortmann, Wilhelm 1048

Houben, H. H. 391

Houlihan, Thomas F. 1921

Housman, Lawrence 383

Hovell, E. B. 385

Howard, Brian 789, 942, 1077a

Howarth, Herbert 1051

Howell, Charles Augustus 498

Hrastnik, H. 1052

Hudson, Derek 83

Hughes, John 1958

Hughes, Riley 90, 1775, 1815, 1840, 1873

Hughes, Serge 1776

Hume, S. J. 385

Hunt, Cecil 673

Hunt, Violet 394

Huskisson, Will 758

Hutchens, J. K. 1635, 1959

Hutchinson, Percy 1485

Hutton, Edward 648

Huxley, Aldous 349h, 402, 438, 847c, 1141, 1280

Huxley, Elspeth 1960

Hynes, Sam 1996

Igoe, W. J. 1961, 2056

Ilchester, Earl of 435

Iles, Francis 1472

Isaacs, Neil D. 1363

Isham, Gyles 1057

Isherwood, Christopher 440, 459, 583

J., A. W. 1571

Jack, P. M. 1591

Jackson, J. H. 1688, 1722, 1777

Jackson, Katherine G. 1962

Jacobson, Dan 1963, 1997

James, E. K. 1572

James, Robert Rhodes 911

James, S. B. 1058

Jarrett, Bede 1059

Jarvis, C. S. 461

Jebb, Julian 664-665

Jervis, Steven Alexander
836, 1364

John XXIII, Pope 376

Johnson, Edgar 496

Johnson, Paul 1922

Johnson, Robert V. 1060

Johnston, Edward 523

Johnston, F. C. 1129, 1707

Johnston, Priscilla 523

Jones, Dan 2031

Jones, David 412

Jones, Ernest 1723

Jones, Iva G. 1097

Joost, Nicholas 1741, 1778

Jungmann 989

Kahan, Herbert 450

Kahrmann, Bernd 1620

Kampmann, Theoderich 1002

Karl, Frederick R. 1061

Karsh, Yousef 526

Kassa, Ras 276

Kaufman, Beatrice 1234

Kaufmann, Stanley 2057

Kearful, Frank J. 1463

Kellogg, Gene 1062-1063

Kennebeck, Edwin 825

Kennedy, J. S. 1724

Kenner, Hugh 1064

Kenny, H. A. 1065

Kermode, Frank 638, 1066,
1663, 1998

Kerman, Alvin B. 78, 1067-
1068

Kielty, Bernardine 73

Kiely, Robert 2092

Kilcoyne, F. P. 825

King, Richard 1347, 1396

King, Robin 1689

Kingery, R. E. 1725

Kingsmill, Hugh 438

Kinset, J. A. 94

Kipling, Rudyard 551

Kirchhoff, Hermann 1002

Kleine, Don W. 1069

Knox, Oliver 1070-1071

Knox, Ronald 42, 49, 53, 336,
353, 355, 356, 479, 520, 534,
596, 619, 630, 631, 631a, 635,
681, 683, 688, 934, 1779

Koechlin, P. 385

Konody, P. G. 1072

Kosok, Heinz 808, 809, 817,
1365, 1621

Kranz, Gisbert 1073-1074

Kunitz, Stanley 1075

Kupersmith, William 648

Labels (A Bachelor Abroad)
6, 20, 195, 196-199, 201,
305, 773, 1393-1406

La Farge, John 1923

La France, Marston 810, 1076,
1622

Lalou, Rene 1636, 1726, 1780,
1841, 1874

Lamb, Dana 453

Lamb, William 438

Lambert, G. W. 2058

Lambotte, Charles 1077

Lancaster, Marie-Jacqueline
1077a

Lancaster, Osbert 485, 870,
1321

Lane, Calvin W. 1079

Lapicque, F. 1080

Large, E. C. 412

Laski, Harold 468

Las Vergnas, Raymond
2059

Laver, James 435

Lawrence, Christie 40

Lawrence, D. H. 383, 637

Lazare, Christopher 1552

Lean, Tangye 1781

Lear, Edward 446

Lechlitner, Ruth 1322

Le Corbusier 386

Legg, L. G. Wickham 522

Lee, Robert 1727

Lehmann, John 1082

Lelotte, F. 1077

Lennartz, Franz 1082a

Leo, J. 1083

Leslie, Shane 1924

Lewis, C. Day 414

Lewis, C. S. 631, 1002

Lewis, E. L. 1637

Lewis, Herbert Clyde 415

Lewis, Rosa 56

Lewis, Wyndham 392, 1084,
1279

Linck, Charles E. 802, 811-
814, 822, 837, 1093-1094,
1366

Lindley, R. 1842

Linkletter, Eric 430, 1095-1096,
1431

Linscott, R. W. 1375

Lips, Julius 414

Lister, R. F. 1088

Little Learning, A 36, 378,
2037-2083

Loban, Walter 791

Long, Richard A. 1097

Longford, Edward, Earl of
364

Longford, Lady 672

Lorda Alaiz, F. M. 1098

Lorentz, Pare 1397

Love Among the Ruins 28, 29, 78, 147, 3491, 775, 1808-1811

"Love in the Slump" 13, 115

Loved One, The 23, 78, 142, 792a, 1703-1707, 1709, 1711-1739

Loved One, The (film) 1708, 1710

Lowrey, Burling 1999

Lunn, Arnold 1098a, 1099

Lyall, Archibald 441

M., C. 1100

M., F. 1348

McCarthy, Joseph 528

Macauley, Rose 1103

McCay, Robert D. 838

Mace, Edward 1340

McCoy, Horace 421

Machin, P. F. 1152

McCormick, John 1104

McCullough, J. I. B. 1445

McDonnell, T. P. 2001

McEwen, R. 1876

McGraw, Hugh 436

McHargue, Georgess 80

McInery, T. A. 54

Mack, Maynard 2007

McLaren, Morey 1105

McLaughlin, Richard 825, 1843, 1877, 1926

McNaspy, C. J. 1966

Mac Neice, Louis 419

Mac Shane, Frank 1706

McShea, John J. 80b

Mc Sorley, Joseph 1575, 1638

Mackenzie, Compton 513

Macmillan, Harold 631

Maddocks, Melvin 1875, 2000

Magner, J. A. 1573

Maguire, C. J. 1102

Maillart, Ella 422

Mais, S. P. B. 1376

Makin, William J. 461

Malcolm, A. E. C. 1377

Maloney, J. 1816

"Man Who Liked Dickens, The" 80, 122-123, 791

Mann, Otto 944

Marcus, Steven 1106

Maritain, Jacques 1185

Markovíc, Vida E. 1107

Marlow, Louis 671

Marlowe, Dave 423

Marlowe, Jack 1592

Marquand, John P. 1165

Marriott, Charles 1593

Marsh, Pamela 2060

Marshall, A. J. 426

Marshall, Bruce 1108-1109

Marshall, Howard 1432

Martin, Graham 1110

Martin, Jean 825

Martin, R. L. 1574

Martindale, C. C. 1623,
1803

Martley, A. R. 1151

Mathew, G. 1925, 1964

Matisse, Henri 591, 603,
625

Matters, Leonard 393

Matthews, T. S. 1349

Mattingly, Joseph F. 2093

Maugham, W. Somerset 104,
457, 887

Maurois, Andre 1481

Maxwell, Gavin 1965

Maxwell, William 1433

May, Derwent 1251

Maycock, J. 1242

Mears, Helen 1410

Mehoke, James S. 1111

Meldrum, D. S. 1323

Men at Arms 26, 1719-1801

Menelik 207

Menen, Aubrey 1742

Meriwether, James R. 980

Merton, Thomas 43, 45, 341,
1257

Metzger, Joseph 1112

Mexico: An Object Lesson.
See *Robbery Under Law*

Meyer, Heinrich 1113

Migeon, G. 385

Mikes, George 1114

Mill, John Stuart 565

Miller, D. J. V. Hamilton 779

Miller, John 486

Miller, Kenneth 825

Miller, Max 421

Mr. Loveday's Little Outing
13, 1523-1531

"Mr. Loveday's Little Outing"
(story) 13, 24, 29, 82, 128,
129, 146

Mitford, Jessica 550, 1116

Mitford, Nancy (Mrs. Peter Rodd)
98, 99, 344, 349k, 452, 535,
1117

Molas, Nicolas de 115, 224

Molt, C. C. and E. M. 749

Monod, Sylvere 1122

Montgomery, John 792

Mooney, Harry J. 1051

Moore, Brian 2061

Moore, Doris Langley 677

Moore, Geoffrey 1844

Moran, D. 385

More, Sir Thomas 613-614

Moriarity, Henry C. 73

Moriarty, F. 1804

Morris, A. S. 1728

Morris, Alice 1782

202

Morris, James 554

Mortimer, John 640

Mortimer, Ray 386

Mortimer, Raymond 1253, 1350

Morton, J. B. 436

Mosley, Nicholas 1123, 1128

Moss, Geoffrey 399

Muggeridge, Malcolm 448,
   480, 634, 825, 1124-1127,
   2062

Munn, L. S. 1503, 1639

Murphy, M. 2100

Murray, James G. 1975

Murray, S. W. 1927

Muskett, Netta 420

Naipaul, V. S. 548

Nasibu, General 284

Neame, A. J. 1123, 1128

Neill, D. G. 1129, 1707

Nemoianu, Virgil 1129a

Nesbitt, L. M. 397, 403

Nettesheim, Josefine 1130

Newby, Eric 51

Newnham, Anthony 1131

Nichols, Beverley 444, 1132-
   1134

Nichols, James W. 817, 1135

Nicolson, Harold 436, 1136,
   1398

Nicolson, Nigel 1136

Nicolson, Robert 450

Nils, Blair 1446

Ninety-Two Days 10, 20, 218-
   223, 225, 1442-1458

Nott, Kathleen 1137

Oakes, Philip [Atticus] 1138

Oboler, E. M. 1901

O'Brian, John 1928

O'Brien, John A. 70

O'Brien, Kate 445, 1594

O'Connor, Frank 1817

O'Connor, W. V. 825

O'Donnell, Donat [pseud. of
   Conor Cruise O'Brien] 857,
   1139-1140, 1878

O'Donovan, Patrick 1929, 2002

O'Faolain, Sean 1141

Officers and Gentlemen 30, 148,
   1829-1862

O'Gorman, F. 1845

Olander, Kathleen 495

Oldmeadow, Ernest 1143, 1434-
   1435, 1473

Oliver, Laurence 674

"On Guard" 13, 24, 29, 83,
   127

Onions, A. R. [Berta Ruck]
   1145

*Open Letter to His Eminence the
   Cardinal Archbishop of West-
   minister, An* 9

Oppell, Horst 1621

Ordeal of Gilbert Pinfold, The
   31, 354, 1863-1897
Orwell, George   470, 1147,
   1690
Orwell, Sonia   1147
Osborne, John   560, 561,
   1148
"Out of Depth"   13, 84, 124
P., T.   1486
Pakenham, Lord Frank   1055,
   1154-1155
Pakenham, Pansy   767
Pakenham, Simona   543
"Palinurus" (Cyril Connolly)
   324, 469
Paltock, Robert   384
Pares, Richard   726, 727,
   1156
Parker, Agnes Miller   430
Parker, Kenneth   1157
Parkes, H. B.   1411, 1576
Pasternak, Boris   1002
Patmore, Derek   1158
Patterson, I. M.   1159
Paulding, Gouverneur   1752
Pearson, Hesketh   437
Pearson, Kenneth   1160
Peden, William   74
Pegeril, Daniel   541
"Period Piece"   13, 24, 29
Petersen, C.   1729

Phelan, Paul J.   79, 86
Phelps, Gilbert   871
Phillips, Gene D.   1624, 2094
Picasso, Pablo   591
Pick, John   1810
Pickrel, Paul   1783, 1818,
   1930, 2003
Pine, Julian   430
Platter, Thomas   426
Plomer, William   1474, 2064
Plunkett-Greene, Babe   1021
Portheim, Paul Cohen   416
Ponsonby, Elizabeth   1021
Poore, Charles   1931, 1967
Posse-Brazdova, Amelie   395
Powell, Anthony   530, 546,
   1163a
Powell, Dilys   1708
Powers, J. F.   477, 510, 1909,
   2065
Prat, Marcella   404
P. R. B.   2
Prescott, Orville   1165, 1640,
   1730, 2004-2005, 2066
Price, Martin   1879
Price, R. G. G.   2006
Priestley, J. B.   354, 462
Prior, Charles   434
Pritchett, V. S.   1166-1167, 1378,
   1447, 1553, 2007, 2032, 2067
Prokosch, Frederick   427

204

Prouse, Derek 1710

Pryce-Jones, Alan 64, 392, 1171, 1595, 2033, 2068-2069

Pryce-Jones, David 1664

Pudney, John 87

Pusateri, L. 1819

Put Out More Flags 17, 132-133, 586, 1585-1605

Quennell, Peter 392, 504, 531, 1172-1174, 1324, 1379, 1475, 1487, 1526

Quinn, P. F. 1820

Quinton, Anthony 2008

R. R. 1314

Raffa, W. G. 387

Rago, Henry 1504

Rahv, Philip 76

Rajan, B. 1190

Ransome, John Crowe 1139

Ratigan, Joseph W. 80b

Raven, Simon 825, 2009, 2101

Ray, Cyril 72, 1071, 1175

Raymond, John 1176, 1753, 1784, 1880

Raynal, Richard 47

Re, Arundell del 1309

Ready, W. 1968, 2010

Redman, B. R. 1505, 1731

Reed, Henry 1641

Rees, Goronwy 1253

Reeves, James 616

Reinhardt, Kurt F. 1177

Reitlinger, Gerald 461

Remote People (They Were Still Dancing) 7, 20, 90, 1407-1421

Restain, K. M. 2102

Reynolds, Horace 1821

Richardson, Maurice 1846

Richardson, Tony 1636

Richel, A. J. 80

Riesner, Dieter 1203

Robbery Under Law (Mexico: An Object Lesson) 16, 316-320, 1570-1584

Robinson, J. K. 817

"Robot" 1311

Rodoconachi, C. P. 438

Rolo, Charles J. 1180-1182, 1691, 1732, 1754, 1847, 1881

Ronald Knox (Monsignor Ronald Knox) 32, 1905-1951

Roos, Hans-Dieter 1183

Rootham, Jasper 471

Rope, H. 1932

Ross, Leonard O. 432

Ross, Mary 1351

Rosetti, Dante Gabriel 189, 394, 401, 478, 572, 788

Rossetti, His Life and Works 3, 1318-1336

Rosten, Leo 525
Rothenstein, William 549
Rousseau, Jean-Jacques 565
Rovere, Richard H. 528,
 1755
Rowse, A. L. 414, 1184
Ruhl, Arthur 1448
Ruskin, John 495, 502
Russell, Bertrand 383
Russell, John 1185
Russell, Leonard 85, 95
Rutherford, Andrew 551,
 2095
Rutter, Owen 415
Ryan, H. F. 1711
Ryan, S. 2011
Ryan, T. C. 660
S., E. 1380
S., M. 1506
S., M. A. 1312
Sackville-West, V. 433
St. John, John 2096
St. Simon, Louis 565
Saki (H. H. Munro) 41
Salamon 385
Sale, Roger 2012
Saltmarshe, Christopher 1187
Sandoz, M. 415
Sarton, May 1882
Sartre, Jean-Paul 1111
Sassoon, Siegfried 431

Saunders, Hilary A. St. George
 322, 1189
Saurat, D. 591
Savage, D. S. 1190
Schäfer, Jürgen 842a
Schaper, Edzard 1002
Schlüter, Kurt 842a, 1191
Schmid, Peter 1193
Schwartz, Delmore 1785
Schwed, Peter 76
Schwinn, L. 1786
Scoop 15, 86, 1544-1569
Scott-King's Modern Europe 21,
 85, 140, 140a, 1682-1702
Secker, Martin 476
Segal, Mark 1399
Seidler, Manfred 1201-1203
Selassie, Haile 204-214, 216,
 227-228, 231-304
Semple, H. E. 2097
Servotte, Herman 1205
Sewell, Elizabeth 1206
Seymour, Beatrice Kean 383,
 719
Shakespeare, William 105, 177,
 559, 703, 1207-1210
Shanahan, W. J. 2070
Shanks, Edward 1325
Shaw, George Bernard 1010
Shawe-Taylor, Desmond 1554
Sheed, W. 1933

Sheehan, Edward 1211-1212
Sheevin, J. B. 1213
Shepherd, L. 1934
Shepperd, L. C. 1787
Sherman, Beatrice 1476
Sherry, John 1969
Shrapnel, Norman 821, 1788,
  1848, 1883
Sillitoe, Alan 1970
Sinclair, Gordon 397
Sissons, Michael 82
Sitwell, Edith 429, 553,
  1082
Sitwell, Sir Osbert 68, 349b-c,
  472, 1082, 1215
Sitwell, Sacheverell 400, 447,
  1082
Skerle, Liselotte 839
Slade, L. 1789
Smith, Bernard 1381
Smith, Bradford 1756
Smith, Lady Eleanor 668,
  789, 872, 1216-1225
Smith, G. 385
Smith, R. D. 1733
Smith, William J. 1971-1972
Snape, H. C. 1935
Snow, C. P. 1110
Soane, Sir John 387
Sobreira, Alberto 1226
Soby, J. T. 1227

"Socrates" 1229
Sonnenfeld, Albert 1230
Soskin, William 1555
Southern, Terry 792a
Southwell, E. M. B. 1151
Southwell, Robert 514, 626
Spark, Muriel 515, 541, 1936
Speaight, Robert 549
Spectorsky, A. C. 1642
Spender, J. A. 425
Spender, Stephen 486, 583,
  1231, 1231a
Spiel, Hilde 1232
Spoerri, Erika 1712
Spring, Howard 462
Squire, J. C. 1326
Stack, K. G. 1790
Staley, Thomas F. 1051, 1233
Stanford, Derek 1234
Stanley, Lord 567
Stark, Freya 432
Starkie, Walter 449
Steer, G. L. 410
Steggert, F. 1822
Stella, Maris 1937
Stepinac 611
Stern, G. B. 1235
Stevenson, Lionel 1236
Stewart, J. W. 1477
Stewart, Neil 431
Stone, Geoffrey 1537

Stone, Linton 1713

Stopes, Marie C. 1237

Stopp, Frederick J. 825,
1238-1241, 1625, 1743,
1884, 2098

Storrs, Sir Ronald 433

Strachey, Julia 1692

Stratford, Philip 1241a,
2071

Straus, Ralph 1242-1243,
1352, 1382, 1400

Stravinsky, Igor 932

Strong, L. A. G. 1247, 1436

Stürzl, Erwin 1245

Sudley, Lord 48

Sugrue, Thomas 1643, 1670

Suhnel, Rudolf 1203

Sullivan, Richard 1507, 1757,
1791, 1823, 1849, 2013, 2103

Sutcliffe, Denham 1693

Sutro, John 1247

Swinnerton, Frank 1383, 1412

Sword of Honour 37, 2084-
2107 See Also *Men at Arms;
Officers and Gentlemen; Unconditional Surrender*

Sykes, Christopher 44, 413,
473, 497, 604, 826, 1249-
1253, 1850, 1938

Sykes, Gerald 1885, 1902

Sylvester, Harry 1758

Symonds, R. W. 547

Symons, Arthur 387

Symons, Julian 1254

Szala, Alina 1626

T., H. M. 1328

Tactical Exercise 29, 1812-
1828

"Tactical Exercise" (story;
see also "The Wish") 29,
31, 139, 153

Tait, Stephen 427

Talbot, C. H. 527

Talbot, Francis X., S. J.
979, 1255

Tallman, Robert 791

Taylor, Rachel A. 1327

Teiling, William 414

Temple, Phillips 1256

Teresa, Saint 631a

Tennant, Stephen 433

Theall, B. 817

Therese, Sister M. 1257

They Were Still Dancing See
Remote People

Thomas, Lowell 395

Thompson, B. 1805

Thompson, Dunstan 1596

Thornton, Philip 419

Tichy, Herbert 453

Tindall, William York 1258

Tito, Marshall 492, 610-612

Todd, Dorothy 386

Todd, Olivier 1259

Tomkins, J. M. S. 842a

Tomlinson, H. M. 400

Tosser, Yvon 815

Tourist in Africa 33, 363, 366, 1952-1983

Tourtellot, A. B. 1556

Toynbee, Philip 2014

Toynbee, Terence de Vere 821

Tracy, Honor 1262

Trappes-Lomax, Michael 619

Traynor, John 2015

Tree, Viola 1263-1264

Trevelyan, G. E. 412

Trevor-Roper, Hugh 613-614, 628, 628a-b

Trilling, Diana 1644

Tshiffely, A. F. 437

Turner, Reggie 552

Tysdahl, Bjørn 1265

Ulanov, Barry 1266

Ullman, James Ramsey 453

Unconditional Surrender (The End of the Battle) 34, 150, 151, 1984-2028

Undset, Sigrid 1073

Unwin, Rayner 495

Van Druten, John 449

Vann, Gerald 1577

Van Zeller, Dom Hubert 1274-1275

Varma, Devendra P. 517

Verschoyle, Derek 1557

Vidal, Gore 2016

Vile Bodies 5, 63, 88, 114, 772, 791a, 1363-1392

Vinci, Count 270-272, 278

Von Puttkamer, Annemarie 1277

Voorhees, Richard J. 1278, 2099

Vota, Lorenzo 59

Vredenburgh, Joseph 1627

W., A. S. 1558

W., E. 1597

Wadia, A. S. 393

Wagner, Geoffrey 1279

Wagner, Linda Welshimer 1280

Waife, Geraldine 750, 760

Wain, John 350, 622

Walbridge, E. F. 1824, 1886

Walker-Smith, Derek 1527

Wall, Barbara 1281

Wall, Bernard 1282

Wall, Mervyn 826

Wallis, Alfred 589

Wallis, David Hudson 890

Walsh, J. 1825

Walton, E. L. 1528

Ward, W. R. 554

Wardman, Lawrence B. 1384

Wasson, Richard 1464

Watts, Richard 1671

Waugh in Abyssinia 14, 20, 299-304, 1532-1543

Waugh, Alec 61, 188, 200, 381-382, 761, 770, 780, 826, 1163, 1286-1288, 2072

Waugh, Arthur 374, 763, 1163, 1289-1291

Waugh, Auberon 1292

Waugh, Evelyn Suppositious works by 1046, 1197, 1204, 1269, 1270, 1277

Waugh, Evelyn Gardner 998, 1030, 1162, 1263

Waugh, Laura 972, 1260

Webster, Harvey Curtis 1293

Wecter, Dixon 1714

Weeks, Edward 1645, 1792, 2017

Weintraub, S. 2073

Welcome, John 88

Wells, H. G. 456

Wells, Joel 88, 1293a, 1294

Welzl, Jan 391

Went, Stanley 1385

Wermuth, P. C. 825

West, Douglas 1529

West, Paul 1294a

West, Rebecca 1295, 1386, 1413

Westminster, Loelia, Duchess of 544

Weston, William 46

Wheatley, D. 80

Wheatley, George A. 1296

Wheeler, Gordon 1906

When the Going Was Good 20, 1667-1681

Whicher, G. F. 1694

Whineray, B. B. 547

White, Antonia 481

White, W. R. 1759, 1826, 1851

Whitridge, Arnold 1329

Whittingten-Egan, R. 816

Wicklow, Earl of (See Lord Clonmore) 50, 821, 1297-1298

Wilde, Oscar 215

Wiley, Paul 817

Willett, John 1341

Williams, Clare 426

Williams, E. T. 522

Willis, K. T. 1672, 1695

Willmering, H. 1806

Wills, Garry 537, 1973

Wilmot, Charles 659

Wilson, Angus 489, 640, 1191, 1299, 1939

Wilson, Colin 1300

Wilson, Edmund 1301, 1508, 1646

Wind, Herbert W. 76

Wine in Peace and War 22

"Winner Takes All" 13, 24, 29, 130

Winter, J. Keith 670

Winwar, Frances 401

"Wish, The" (See "Tactical Exercise") 87, 138

Wodehouse, P. G. 350, 365, 407, 460, 512, 622

Wolfe, Humbert 383, 751

Wolff, J. 2074

Wood, Frederick 2018

Woodburn, John 1673, 1696, 1734

Woodcock, George 1302

Woodruff, Douglas 518, 604, 681, 1303, 2075

Woollcott, Alexander 77, 1304

Wooton, Carl W. 841, 1628

Work Suspended 18, 131, 134-135

Work Suspended and Other Stories 24

World of Evelyn Waugh 1898-1904

World to Come, The 1

Worth, Harry 1160

Wright, Cuthbert 1598

Xavier, St. Francis 100, 349e

Young, B. A. 1974

Young, G. M. 430

Zipprich, M. H. 1793

Zuleuta, Marie-Louise de 847a, 1292